Youniquely Woman

KAY ARTHUR
EMILIE BARNES
DONNA OTTO

HARVEST HOUSE PUBLISHERS

EUGENE, OREGON

Cover by Koechel Peterson & Associates, Inc., Minneapolis, Minnesota

YOUNIQUELY WOMAN
Copyright © 2008 by Kay Arthur, Emilie Barnes, and Donna Otto
Published by Harvest House Publishers
Eugene, Oregon 97402
www.harvesthousepublishers.com

Library of Congress Cataloging-in-Publication Data
   Arthur, Kay
   Youniquely woman / Kay Arthur, Emilie Barnes, Donna Otto.
      p. cm.
   ISBN-13: 978-0-7369-1726-1
   ISBN-10: 0-7369-1726-8
   1. Christian women—Religious life. 2. Christian women—Conduct of life. I. Barnes, Emilie. II. Otto, Donna. III. Title.
   BV4527.A785 2008
   248.8'43—dc22

                                     2007034934

Printed in the United States of America

08 09 10 11 12 13 14 15 / VP-SK / 11 10 9 8 7 6 5 4 3 2 1

*To the extraordinary, Younique Women
who gave us courage.*

*Emilie: To Mama Irene, Florence Littauer,
and Evelyn Friedman*

*Donna: To Jeannette Bakke, Sylvia Bjork, Trish Crace,
didi Foss, Mardel, Luster, Marie Petersen, Pauline Robinson,
Allyne Rubel, and Mildred Van Liew*

*Kay: To each and every one of you who came to our
Youniquely Woman "Finishing Schools."
You were superlative students, and
we're so proud of you!*

Kay, Emilie, and Donna

Acknowledgments

When three strong solo voices sing together in a book like this, you either end up with harmony or noise. As we worked together on this amazing project, we found wonderful chemistry and fun together. We hope that's harmony. Kay sings with her characteristic prophetic, scriptural soprano while Emilie and Donna add the practical and helpful melody of encouragement. It works because we are sisters in faith with a zeal to tell women about God's faithfulness in our lives and what it takes to be "youniquely woman."

Of course we had a great team of accompanists. Our heartfelt thanks go to Bob Hawkins Jr., who first saw the vision of Youniquely Woman and faithfully carried it through. He is the one who heard the music. We also thank Carolyn McCready and LaRae Weikert of Harvest House who conducted us creatively through the project as only gifted sisters in Christ can.

We'd also like to acknowledge those who were instrumental in helping to execute our vision for the Youniquely Woman conferences:

> To Kim Rock and her team at PMI who gave their all in organizing, co-coordinating, and hostessing our Youniquely Woman events. And to the team who daily discipled the women who came to the Youniquely Woman events, teaching them how to discover Truth for themselves and then teach it to their children: Tommye Hammel, Beverly Mealor, Gloria James, Jan Priddy, BJ Lawson, and Janna Arndt. And to the HBC staff for your work in helping to create the Youniquely Woman curriculum.

And finally, if there is truly harmony here, it is due to the labors of our wonderful friend and editor, Larry Libby. Thank you, Larry, for helping our voices come together.

Listen to the music.

Contents

One

Living Intentionally

A Goal and a Legacy

Kay

"Knowing what I know now…" Have you heard older people talk like that? "Knowing what I know now…

- I would have done things better…
- I would have grabbed that opportunity…
- I would have reacted differently…
- I would have run from that place as fast as I could…
- I would have stayed in school…
- I would have married someone else…
- I would have been more patient and kind…
- I would have spent more time with my son…my daughter."

Certainly there are many things I would like to do over and years I'd like to live over:

- I would shun those destructive paths I allowed myself to walk.
- I would hold my tongue and not speak those unloving words.
- I would guard my thoughts and rein in my dreams.
- I wouldn't have divorced my husband.

- I would have asked my sons how they were feeling and focused more on them than on trying to find a husband.

I've often thought I would write a book and title it *Hindsights for Insight*. But that's life, isn't it, dear one? Once the days and hours and moments have slipped through our fingers, we can't go back and alter anything—as much as we long to do that. All the wishing, wanting, and daydreaming in the world can't change that fact. We can't do anything about "then," but we can do something about "now."

That's why Donna, Emilie, and I put together our *Youniquely Woman* events, and that's why we've written this book. We can't return to those years of young womanhood. We can't recapture those seasons when we were young wives and mothers with little ones. But God is so good, so kind, that He's given us *this* opportunity to share with you what we've learned (sometimes through hard experience) and what we would do differently. In other words, the book you hold in your hands can literally save you from years of regret.

From Donna

Abraham was the father/leader of the Hebrew family/nation. He helped God change history. Is God calling you to be the Abraham of your family by implementing changes in the present that will positively impact the future for your family?

Actually, it's even more personal for me.

I've always wanted a daughter. Now, I love my sons and wouldn't trade them for anything. But I've always longed for the joy and companionship of a daughter, for the privilege of discipling a daughter to become a godly woman. And now I have that opportunity…with you! (Thank You, Lord, for Your incredible kindness!)

I was something of a free-spirited woman who can, as the expression goes, fly by the seat of her pants. I could…and I did…but I wish I hadn't. A divorced mother of two sons and longing for love, I fell into immorality. But then I was gloriously saved by Jesus Christ at age 29. Eventually I remarried after my first husband committed suicide. And now that I am an older woman (with a young woman trapped inside my body!), I wish I'd been far more intentional as a wife, mother, and grandmother.

I'm deliberately using the word "intentional." It's not a word you see very often. When I speak of living in an intentional way, I mean *living on purpose.* Living a life directed by goals and principles and precepts so I will get the most out of life and have few regrets in the years to come. And that's what this book is all about.

God has taught the three of us—Donna, Emilie, and me—much from His Word through the

From Emilie

My growing up years weren't lived intentionally. My family was happy if we had money to buy food because my father died when I was 11. It was very hard for my mama. Even when Daddy was living, he was gone 90 percent of the time. I praise God for protecting me from going in an unhealthy direction. Live intentionally for Christ!

years. Yes, we've experienced heartache and tribulation in our lives, just as Jesus told us clearly we would. At times the hurt has run deep, but His grace has been lavish…altogether sufficient—no, beyond sufficient…extravagant! How I love the words of the apostle Peter:

> His divine power has granted to us everything pertaining to life and godliness, through the true knowledge of Him who called us by His own glory and excellence (2 Peter 1:3).

When it comes to being a woman, a daughter of the living God, we are called to excellence. And this is our desire for you. We want you to be like the woman described in Proverbs 31:29: "Many daughters have done nobly, but you excel them all." And how do you achieve excellence? By living intentionally. And by remembering that God's divine power makes it possible.

Yes, I would be less than honest if I didn't admit I was oblivious to the powerful concept of living intentionally for a long time. The years slipped by, and I was so caught up with the daily pressures of "just living" that I never took a long look at where my habits and my ways were leading me. There's an old saying, "What I am to be, I am now becoming." As with many such sayings, it contains truth and error. What it's really saying is that the choices I am making *today* will have a direct bearing on the shape of my life down the road. The path I choose *now* leads to where I'm going. That's so true. The apostle Paul says much the same thing in Galatians 6:7-8:

> Do not be deceived, God is not mocked; for whatever a man sows, this he will also reap. For the one who sows to his own flesh will from the flesh reap corruption, but the one who sows to the Spirit will from the Spirit reap eternal life.

But it's also true that there is both immediate and long-term benefits of choosing the right paths, the right sources of wisdom...*and these choices can absolutely flood our lives with the grace, kindness, mercy, and bounty of our God who loves us with all His great heart.*

Donna, Emilie, and I are going to admit our wrong turns and unwise choices...so you don't have to repeat them. So please listen carefully, dear one. Check what we teach you with the precepts of God's Word, and see if it lines up with truth. Then live accordingly. And when you stumble, get back up, ask God's forgiveness, and keep moving forward.

Amelia and Susanna: Their Legacy

Just for a paragraph or two, I want to reach back into history to tell you of two ordinary women who lived intentionally. By fearing God—respecting Him, trusting Him, and ordering their lives accordingly—these women left all of us a rich legacy.

Listen to the intentionality of Amelia Hudson Boomhall, who lived in 1875:

> I made it a rule to take my children one at a time into my room, and having been careful to see that they were comfortably

seated, I would say, "I am going to talk to Jesus." And then before my child, I would pour out my soul to Him. Oh how precious are the memories of little pinafores lifted to wipe my eyes, or the sound of sweet little voices saying, "Don't cry, Mother."[1]

If God said, "Kay, you can have a 'do-over,'" I would pray more purposefully for my children and my husband. But you and I can't go back. We can only do from this point on.

The second woman who comes to mind is Susanna Wesley, who lived in the 1700s. Susanna's husband was a God-fearing man and a pastor. He never earned very much money, and the little he did earn he mismanaged. At one point he was even threatened with being thrown into debtors' prison.

And his was no modern family with 2.1 children. In the course of their marriage, Susanna gave birth to *19 children,* 9 of whom died as infants, including two sets of twins. Because her husband traveled so much on church business, Susanna was often left to care for her large family alone. She raised her children with strong intentionality.

From Donna

It is never too late to change. You always have the present! The opportunity to harvest wisdom from your past is a golden gift to be prized.

Although her marriage wasn't what women would dream of and some of her children didn't follow the Lord, Susanna raised two sons whose names will forever be remembered in the annals of Christian history. Generations have sung the doctrines of the Christian faith set to music in the hymns of John and Charles Wesley. Do you recognize this one written in 1739 by Charles?

O for a thousand tongues to sing
My great Redeemer's praise,
The glories of my God and King,
The triumphs of His grace!

The Wesley brothers were bellows in the hands of God and ignited the smoldering embers of Christendom, bringing revival fires to a church languishing in dead religious traditions. Their followers became known as "Methodists," and their influence shaped the history of England and the United States.

How did this happen? Their mother, Susanna, raised them with intentionality, making the priorities of God and family paramount in her life and her children's lives.

A married woman can have no higher callings than being a godly wife and mother. The world will tell you that driving race cars, piloting jumbo jets, climbing the corporate ladder, and earning piles of money will bring the most satisfaction. And for a single woman those goals may certainly be within reach. But a married woman who loves her husband, raises her children to know the Lord, and makes her home into a beautiful, peaceful sanctuary in this hostile world…that, my daughter, is the best of the best.

The Bible tells us it's possible to live life with excellence, to live an uncommon life, and to be used of God beyond our expectations and dreams. Let's explore and experience those things!

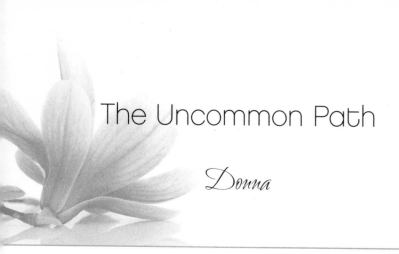

The Uncommon Path

Donna

In these days of "please yourself at any cost," living with intentionality might be called "choosing an uncommon path." Writer Fredrick Buechner once said, "My assumption is that the story of any one of us is, in some measure, the story of all of us." Our stories as Christian women—daughters, wives, mothers, aunts, and grandmothers—have common elements. In a broad sense, each life is like another. At different points in our lives, most of us have had similar hopes, goals, and dreams.

All of us begin our journeys with aspirations and desires. But somewhere along the way the trails separate. The common woman moves into a common life. The uncommon woman, however, takes another path and becomes all that *God* intended her to be. "The common begin, but the uncommon finish." That's one of the thoughts I've repeated to myself through the years. And what is the reason paths separate? What causes one woman to accept an ordinary path into an ordinary life and another to end her story with great fulfillment and joy?

The path divider is courage.

Courageous choices at the crossroads of life separate uncommon life stories from everyday ones. I'm not talking about people living perfect lives. That's impossible. My own story includes a devastating divorce. And while it is still the most painful part of my life (because I know God hates divorce), it's become the driving force behind my passion and my ministry. None of us want to be wounded, hurt, or crushed by circumstances. But the positive side is that we have a God so big and mighty He can and will use even hurtful things to accomplish His purposes.

From Emilie

Women, put your life in the hands of God and allow Him to walk with you each step of the way.

It's safe to conclude that God has allowed your pain—your most difficult circumstances—to stir passion in your heart and refine His purposes for your life. My pain motivated me to seek God, who gave me the courage to look beyond the pain and find something positive to do with the lessons I learned. I've spent more than 25 years of my adult life teaching, training, and leading young women through an organization I founded called "Homemakers By Choice." The concepts of courage and commitment weave their way through everything I teach.

For instance, I continually emphasize the need to be women of our word. When we say yes to something, we need to stand behind that choice. When a woman marries and pledges herself to remain faithful in sickness and in health, till death separates her from her husband, I encourage her to keep that pledge. The pain I endured through my divorce has made me passionate about committing to a marriage relationship through thick and thin.

Staying true to our promises and commitments takes courage. But guess what? So does making needed changes in our lives. Most of us enjoy a feeling of security, and we like to surround ourselves with the comfort of familiar places and things. There's nothing wrong with such desires...unless the Lord is calling you to take a step of growth, a step of faith, a step into the unknown. Only an abiding trust in the Lord Jesus allows us to leap confidently across a chasm of the unknown so we can jump into His waiting arms.

Just recently I learned a bit about leaping.

A Jump in the Jungle

Adventure is second nature to my husband. For him, the very word means charging into daunting, uncharted territory. The riskier the adventure the better. These exploits have included arduous hikes of 60 miles or more over wet and uneven terrain, dangerous climbs along steep cliffs, and even having a boat capsize in the Pacific Ocean!

So guess whose idea it was to travel to Costa Rica for our vacation? (What's wrong with Maui?) I have to admit, however, that the land was truly beautiful with its amazing array of exotic animals.

One morning my husband persuaded me to experience something called a "zip line" out in the rain forest. Knowing my husband, I was pretty sure the experience was going to stretch me. I just didn't realize how far!

The day began with a climb up a five-story staircase until we were in the highest treetops. That seemed like plenty of adventure for me…I could have turned back right then and headed to the hotel for a cup of tea and been perfectly content. But it was just the beginning. I soon found myself being strapped into a harness attached to a cable that stretched so far into the distance I couldn't see the end of it. As soon as this was completed, I was escorted to the edge of a platform (*plataforma* in Costa Rica).

The next thing I heard was "Jump!"

Jump? Jump where? Landing on what? I thought. *Not me! I'm not about to leave this platform—plataforma—or whatever it is.*

After a few minutes of protests, I discovered there was no way down or out until I left that platform. It was jump or nothing. So I jumped. Well, actually I agreed to be pushed. The animal kingdom has never before or since heard a louder or more piercing scream than I delivered that day zipping over the treetops. After what seemed a lifetime, I found myself landing on another platform.

Whew! I thought. *That's that. I did it!* I jumped into nothing and zipped down the line. Not wanting to offend my grinning Costa Rican guide, I politely said, "Thank you, that was nice" and looked for the exit. He shook his head, still smiling. "No, senora," he said. "Fourteen more plataformas!"

Eventually (since I lived to tell this story) I successfully completed the jungle zip line experience. And do you want to know something funny? After the sheer terror of the first four or five plataformas, I actually began to enjoy myself!

Every one of us faces plataformas in life—and many more than 14! Are you standing on one right now? Yours will be different from mine, or your sister's, or your mother's, or your daughter's. But the common element in all of them is the courage needed to trust our God and take those leaps.

The book you hold in your hands is a plataforma. You will learn things in these pages that offer you opportunities to make significant choices and changes. If you rise to the challenge, you'll be on the road to becoming a "younique" woman of God. The easy choice is to simply read this book, file the information in your mind under "interesting thoughts," and never do anything more. The difficult choice—the choice that will put you on an uncommon path—is trusting the Lord and taking the leaps we suggest.

The Plataformas of Spiritual Discipline

"Discipline." I make no apology for mentioning the "d" word here. My life is riddled with started and aborted attempts at spiritual disciplines. To follow through and actually incorporate these into your life will initiate wonderful changes that may positively shape and impact the rest of your days on this side of heaven. But no one is saying it will be easy. John W. Frye asks, "What is a spiritual discipline?" Then he answers, "It is simply a human activity that creates a space or setting for God to work." A space or setting? Couldn't we also say "platform"? To become an uncommon woman you want and need to create these spaces for God to work.

The spiritual disciplines of Bible study, prayer, fasting, solitude, serving, and detachment (letting go of what keeps us from intimacy with Jesus) can become a way of life for a younique woman. As you continue reading *Youniquely Woman,* you'll discover suggestions and specific helps for allowing and building spaces for God to work in your daily life.

Yes, it takes courage to be intentional in your life.

It takes courage to choose an uncommon path.

C.S. Lewis writes, "Courage is not simply one of the virtues, but the form of every virtue at the testing point." Courage is necessary to discover God's design for you.

It takes courage to stick to your commitments...and even more courage to choose additional commitments that will shape and change you.

It takes courage to stand up and stand out as a unique creation of God.

It takes courage to be the woman God created you to be as you live through each life season and seek to please God.

It takes courage not to compare yourself with women in movies, magazines, and books.

It takes courage to swim against the strong current of popular culture.

It takes courage not to base your life on competition or defensiveness.

Living a courageous, character-driven life is uncommon. There are thrills and excitements in being youniquely woman...a woman created in the image of God as His last, best, and surely most complex creation. I hope and pray you'll find and appreciate the specific nuances that make you different from any other woman in the world.

As older women, it is clear to Kay, Emilie, and me that God's specific plan can be known and lived out with individuality and freedom. As the authors of this book, we celebrate God's unique design and touch on your life.

A Shining Example

Recently I attended the funeral of a courageous woman who lived to be 100 years old. Mildred was mother to 4, grandmother to 22, and great-grandmother to 26. She also offered mother/grandmother relationships to many nonfamily members, including me.

One of 12 children, she lived in rural America during the early part of the twentieth century. Mildred's daily life was filled with hard work. Her husband died early in the marriage, leaving her a widow for more than 40 years.

At Mildred's funeral I watched and listened to a parade of multicultural, multigenerational men and women speak of her influence in their lives, of the legacy she left.

In the 1950s, when women like Donna Reed, Harriet Nelson, and Loretta Young were portrayed on TV wearing aprons and dusting coffee tables, Mildred was partnering with her husband in a business venture. She helped start, fund, and organize a mission in Korea that saved thousands of unwanted orphans. Her life was diverse. She wasn't afraid to pursue her special calling on this earth, no matter what the rest of her women friends were doing or thought. And I must add she wasn't always popular for taking such determined stands.

Mildred stood against the tide of her culture, welcoming change and transition. She worked hard without apology, lived frugally, and gave generously. She wasn't afraid to step into the gap to get things done, but at the same time she was regarded as a gracious, gentle, godly woman.

My friend Mildred had an uncommon life and finished well.

I want that too, don't you?

Each day life affords us opportunities to stand up and be counted, to do the unusual and unexpected. Many years ago, after I married David and took the name Otto, I began creating and adapting what I call "Otto's Mottoes." Clear, simple, memorable, credible sayings that help me stay on the course I've chosen. Here's one:

> Right is always right no matter how few people are doing it, and wrong is always wrong no matter how many people are doing it.

In other words, don't bend the rules to fit *your* needs. There will be many testing points, and with courage comes the willingness to seek and accept change. In his second letter to believers, the apostle Peter sets forth a life-changing concept: "For if these qualities are yours and are increasing, they keep you from being ineffective or unfruitful in the knowledge of our Lord Jesus Christ" (2 Peter 1:8-9).

"Increasing measure." I understand this to mean that even up to the day before I die, I will accept the need for change and seek direction for that change, with the result that I am "ever increasing" in those areas of life that matter most.

Since you've read this far, I assume you have the same desire I have—a desire for sufficient courage to walk an uncommon road through life. So we're on this plataforma together! Are you ready to leap? Let's go!

Two

A Vision for Home

Holy Ground

Donna

The year was 1945, and the young newlyweds had a specific vision of a home. They would build a house together. They found a small piece of property with a narrow-but-wonderful view of Puget Sound…and began to plan their dream house—a modest home with a two-car garage (actually a rather extravagant vision for that post-war era when housing was scarce). The plan was to work on the dream a little at a time. So they bought the lot and saved for the house. They built the garage first to store supplies and have a place to work. Then, to save money, they moved into the garage, portioning the space into small rooms.

Some 55 years later, the now-widowed wife was still living in that converted garage. For a variety of reasons, the dream house never materialized, and trees gradually obscured the view of the Sound. Yet as neighbors and relatives will tell you, that small space served well the family raised there. And to the daughters and grandchildren who traveled back often to visit, that tiny converted garage always felt like a haven of love.

Later, at the mother's funeral, the two daughters marveled at how warm and alive that little garage-house seemed during their growing-up years. Without the presence of their mother, the little space now looked tiny and inadequate. With her it had radiated joy, faith, energy, and warmth. It was within those modest walls that they received large portions of encouragement, grace, and beauty. The converted garage felt as spacious and embracing as the love that lived there. The space their mother made so special always felt—well, like home.

Home. It's a beautiful word to most of us. It speaks of comfort, acceptance, relaxation, and love. It's a warm, safe place to be and a good place to grow up. A place where most of us would love to live, even if we never had those kinds of experiences before.

The title of this chapter is "A Vision for Home," and I believe that vision is one that comes directly from God. As believers we're called to look at our homes the way God sees them—as vital centers to teach His truth and model His ways...*as holy ground.*

Holy Ground

What's the first thing you do when you enter your home after a long day of running errands or keeping appointments or chasing after your kids? I'm talking about that moment after you put down your purse or the groceries but before you check for any messages. If you're like a lot of women I know, you take off your shoes.

Why? Maybe you want to spare the carpet. Or maybe you're on your way to change into running shoes or hiking boots for a workout. Maybe you can't wait to kick off those toe-pinching pumps and savor the luxury of padding around in your bare feet. Or perhaps you've been waiting to slip your toes into some slippers, flip-flops, or comfortable house shoes while you put your feet up and nurse the baby or listen to your kids share what happened in school.

Taking off your shoes. It's such a relaxed, homey thing to do. It's an action you take in a place where you feel safe and accepted. What does taking off your shoes have to do with a "holy ground" vision for home and finding your purpose as a wife and mother? Maybe more than you think.

Encounter in the Desert

Remember the story of Moses and the burning bush? The young

prince was in exile from Egypt, the land of his birth, the land where he'd learned a painful truth: The people who raised him had enslaved and mistreated the people who gave him life.

One day while alone in the wilderness tending his father-in-law's sheep, Moses came upon an amazing sight—a burning bush. But not just any burning bush. The flames licked the leaves and branches of that desert plant, but nothing was actually being consumed. It was a fire in the bush, and yet the bush wasn't on fire.

After 40 years of leading sheep through a monotonous wilderness, *anything* new or interesting was a welcome phenomenon. So Moses walked over to the bush to check it out. As he stared in wonder, he heard the Lord speak: "Remove your sandals from your feet, for the place on which you are standing is holy ground" (Exodus 3:5). God wasn't telling Moses to get comfortable. He was warning him that something important was going on and reminding him to show respect and humility in the presence of something sacred. And the Lord was also plainly telling His servant He had important work for him to do.

I believe the Lord is speaking a similar word to women today who have the joy and responsibility of tending a home and caring for a family. *"Take off your shoes,"* He is saying. *"The place where you are cooking, cleaning, and raising the next generation is indeed holy ground. You are Mine, and your home is part of My plan for changing the world."*

Regardless of who you are, whether you've made the choice to be a stay-at-home mom or work outside the home, whether you're married or single, whether your house is a two-car garage in a desert or a mansion on a hillside...I believe these words are for you. Your home is holy ground because it's where God has chosen to live and do His work.

Does thinking about your home this way make you squirm a little—especially when you think of the piles of laundry in the corner or the dishes in the sink or the way you lost your temper with your children yesterday morning?

I understand your feeling. I've felt that way myself. But at the same time, I've come to cherish the understanding that my home and my family are not only God's gifts to me, but they're also a holy trust. They are central to God's purpose for my life—His chosen vehicles for bringing about the future. Home is a place for me to live and to leave a legacy—to build something lasting on holy ground. That reality has been part of God's plan from the very dawn of creation.

Instead of creating societies with a vast sweep of His mighty arm, God created a single family—a man and a woman. He gave them a home, a special place to live and to be. He gave them responsibility for populating the earth and caring for the rest of creation—with specific roles for each of them. And even after they disobeyed Him and had to leave that garden, the new homes they established continued to be significant in God's plan of redemption.

From Kay

I wish my husband and I had taken the time to write out what we wanted for our home, our children, our lives. What are our family values? What do we want to teach our children? What is allowed and not allowed? What can we do to achieve these goals?

If you do this, keep a journal for evaluation and to pass on to your kids.

Throughout the Old and New Testaments we find the idea that homes are places where souls are nourished and God's ways are taught. A few passages, such as Deuteronomy 6:4-9, state this specifically. Some, such as Proverbs 31 and passages from Paul's epistles, elaborate on the roles and responsibilities of men and women and children in the home. And many others take as a given that God's work in a human life begins at home in loving relationship to a family that lives and works and worships together. In fact, the Bible refers to houses, homes, and dwelling places more than 600 times.

A human dwelling place, a shelter, a home, is a small reflection of the home and shelter we find in God. As Moses wrote, "LORD, you have been our dwelling place in all generations" (Psalm 90:1). In a time of fear and sorrow, Jesus spoke to His troubled men about a home beyond all earthly homes: "In my Father's house are many rooms. If it were not so, would I have told you that I go to prepare a place for you?" (John 14:2).

Home matters to God. And because it matters to Him, it should matter to you. It's the heart of who you are as a wife, a mom, and a daughter of God.

Surely it's important to remember that when God sent His Son into the world, He chose to place Him in the setting of a home and family, a warm place where He could grow in wisdom and stature and favor with God and man. After Jesus embarked on His ministry, though He didn't have a specific place "to lay His head" (Matthew 8:20), He obviously treasured the homes opened to Him. And although He called His disciples away from their homes sometimes and seemed to urge them to break their family ties, a look behind the scenes shows His tender regard for home and family. Why else would He have bothered to work miracles at a wedding, heal Peter's mother-in-law, and make arrangements, while in agony on the cross, for the care of His aging mother?

From the very beginning God has made it clear: Home is holy ground.

Your home is holy ground.

And it's your responsibility, even amid the messes and confusion of daily life, not only to take off your shoes but to also tend the holy flame. As a human being in whom God's Spirit dwells, you have that privilege. As a woman, as a wife, as a mother, you have a special set of gifts and responsibilities. You are called to create and maintain a home environment and atmosphere that reflects God's love, God's hope, God's peace. Quite literally, you build your home on holy ground.

Emilie, Kay, and I encourage you to think about how you relate to your home base, this place where you sleep, wash, pray, train your children, and yes, take off your shoes. We don't want you to forget God's vision for your home. We want to affirm for you the heavenly importance of what you do in your home—whether it's scrubbing toilets or cooking dinner or playing Monopoly with your children. We want to support you whether you're privileged to care for your home and family full time or whether you do it in conjunction with outside work. We want to persuade you to think *intentionally* and *counterculturally* about what it means to be the mood-setter. To create, as Emilie likes to put it, a *welcome home* atmosphere.

Intentional thinking is important for establishing a vision of home because much of our culture has fallen into the assumption that home will "take care of itself." Women used to know better, but I find that many women today are completely unaware that shaping a nurturing home environment— as with any other important endeavor—takes planning, purpose, organization, and time. If we want our homes to be warm and welcoming, if we want to be successful at raising saints for the King, we need to arrange for that to happen. We need to do it on purpose.

I also used the term *countercultural* thinking. I did that because our current culture tends to be absolutely clueless—or even perverse—in the way it views home life, wifely duties, and motherhood. We live in a society that features entire cable channels devoted to "house beautiful," whetting our appetites for homemade bread (with homegrown herbs!) and crisp, fragrant, hand-embroidered sheets. Yet the underlying implication is that we can do all of this in just a few hours in the evening after a hard day at the office.

Our culture makes a lot of noise about "nurturing children," yet deeply distrusts and frequently devalues those who choose to make nurturing their career.

As followers of Christ, no matter what our specific circumstances

---

From Emilie

My childhood home was three little rooms behind my mama's dress shop. A bucket of paint for the walls, a quilt to cover a chipped table, and a candle and a cup of tea brightened the place. This is the home I remember— great love, a calm spirit, and soft music. It was a home, not just three rooms with walls.

or our personal decisions, we need to take a stand against this schizophrenic culture that idealizes and devalues home life. We need to move beyond house beautiful and house status and house drudgery and into the heavenly realm of house holy.

Take off your shoes…because your home can be a gift of safety and comfort and freedom for you and your family. Something can happen there. In fact, it's *supposed* to happen there. Your precious Savior wants to use your life and your work and your roles as a woman, a wife, a mom to change the world.

Take off your shoes and you might even want to roll up your sleeves. The challenging and fulfilling task of being a purposeful woman in a holy home awaits you.

The Heart of Home
David and Donna Otto

There is a wonderful place,
a space so secure and warm,
that all privileged to live there
call it home.

Who holds the heart of this home?

The walls are colored with laughter
and the floors with wall-to-wall memories.
Each space testifies to the
bustling energy and joy of blended lives.

Who holds the heart of this home?

It's more than an address
or a statement of achievement and style.
It's a tender oasis from the storms of daily life,
a place of peace and rest.

Who holds the heart of this home?

Cheerleaders for life dwell here
as do living testimonies for faith.
Imperfect saints work out the walk of wisdom
in the halls of this home.

Who holds the heart of this home?

For every damaged day and sharp defeat
home is the balm for the wound.
For every cutting word and ungracious event,
home is the kindness we crave.

Who holds the heart of this home?

And every bad memory of family and childhood
is swallowed in the embrace of a now happy home.
The time for forgiveness and healing is here
in the sanctuary of home.

Who holds the heart of this home?

So those who build a home instead of a house,
a deliberate and prayer-laced place
rather than a sterile designer's
delight do well.

Who holds the heart of this home?

You hold the heart of this home.

A Pattern for Success

Kay

Home, as Donna said, is not only holy ground, it is also the epicenter of family life—a warm, safe, sheltering place where we can come in from the storms and dangers of the world outside. And that has never been more true than right now. There's no doubt about it—we live in difficult days, among people hostile to those who love God and His Word and scornful of many of the values believers hold dear.

None of this should surprise us. Over 2000 years ago the apostle Paul wrote to a young friend about the very days we're living in right now: "Realize this," he told Timothy, "that in the last days difficult times will come." He went on to describe the kind of people and the kind of attitudes we would be seeing in the world around us. He said,

> Men will be lovers of self, lovers of money, boastful, arrogant, revilers, disobedient to parents, ungrateful, unholy, unloving, irreconcilable, malicious gossips, without self-control, brutal, haters of good, treacherous, reckless, conceited, lovers of pleasure rather than lovers of God, holding to a form of godliness, although they have denied its power (2 Timothy 3:1-5).

Does this sound like ancient history to you? No, it doesn't. It sounds as current as this morning's news.

As the time for the return of Jesus to this world draws near, the Bible tells us the world will be an ever darker and more threatening place. And this is the world where we seek to raise children to love and obey the Lord? What can we do? How can we protect our sons and daughters and provide a safe haven in a world like this? Is it even possible? The answer is a strong *yes*.

You and I, dear daughter, can make our homes a little bit of heaven on earth if we will do all we can to pattern our families and homes after God's home. Where do we find that pattern? It's not going to be on the Internet, talk radio, or afternoon television. You won't find it in the pages of magazines. If we want the pattern for God's home, our reliable, unchanging source is between the covers of the Bible. What a miracle! Here is a book written over thousands of years through the hands and personalities of multiple authors from every walk of life. And yet it is as current and up-to-date as today's page on your day planner. How I love God's Word! It is *life!*

When Moses spoke his last words to the people of Israel, he laid down this important truth: "Take to your heart all the words with which I am warning you today...For it is not an idle word for you; *indeed it is your life*. And by this word you will prolong your days in the land" (Deuteronomy 32:46-47).

For so many today, the Bible is "an idle word." They see it as recitation of religious rules or irrelevant history. If only they understood that following the path of biblical wisdom is life! And as we understand and apply God's precepts on the home, *life* comes into our homes. As we apply His precepts to our marriages, *life* comes into our marriages. This is where you and I can find everything we need to be equipped for every good work we will ever put our hands to. These are God's precepts for life!

In his second letter to Timothy, Paul told the young man that "all Scripture is inspired by God and profitable for teaching, for reproof, for correction, for training in righteousness; so that the man of God may be adequate, equipped for every good work" (2 Timothy 3:16-17). And in Peter's final letter, he assures us that God's "divine power has granted to us everything pertaining to life and godliness, through the true knowledge of Him who called us by His own glory and excellence" (2 Peter 1:3).

Now then, in light of those wonderful promises, let's look at some specific principles that bring us immediate encouragement and help, giving us God's pattern for the family and for our homes.

God Sets the Pattern

First of all, it's a great reassurance to realize that there truly is a pattern for the family.

It isn't random.

It isn't "whatever."

God didn't leave us to wonder or to cast about looking for answers. Our contemporary culture tells us we're simply on our own. A family, they say, is anything we want it to be—no set pattern, no design, no restrictions, no requirements. And by making the definition of family mean everything, they make the family nothing.

But that's *not* what the Bible tells us. Listen to these amazing words from Paul: "For this reason I bow my knees before the Father, from whom every family in heaven and on earth derives its name" (Ephesians 3:14-15). Family life didn't simply evolve; it had a starting place. Whether people choose to acknowledge it or not, *every family on earth derives its name from Father God.* When Adam named all the animals back in the Garden of Eden, that very act of naming showed his authority over them. In the same way, because every family on earth derives its name from God, we understand that He has authority over our families and over our lives. This also indicates that He is the one who sets the template or pattern for family life. If we want to succeed in our marriages, succeed in our families, then it makes sense that we learn what God's pattern is and follow it.

Reason with me for a few minutes. We have been taught to pray, "Our Father who is in heaven" (Matthew 6:9). God is a Father—a Father with a Son! When I'm teaching inductive Bible study, I show students how to mark every reference to God with a triangle. Why that symbol? Because it helps us picture the Trinity—Father, Son, and Holy Spirit.

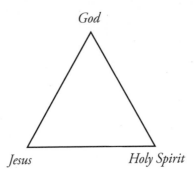

A man and woman united in marriage can also be represented by a triangle—with God at the peak, over all, holding everyone together.

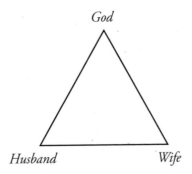

In John 1:12 we read about receiving Jesus and becoming children of God. The Father, the Son, and the Spirit have children...us! We are born into God's family, and we are deeply loved (John 3:5). The Bible tells us that God loved us first, before we ever knew Him. He loved us when we were helpless, godless sinners, and His enemies (1 John 4:10; Romans 5:8). If we've accepted His gift and provision for our sin—His Son—He may discipline us in His love, but we can be assured that nothing will ever separate us from Him or change His love for us (Hebrews 12:10; Romans 8:35-39). He loves us with an everlasting love.

That describes the heart of Father God for His family, for His children. And that is His pattern for *all* families and for *every* home. How like God are we? Do we truly love our children? Or do we love ourselves more than them? Remember, God gave His Son as the ultimate expression of His love. There was no other way to save us, and so He paid the price so you and I can become His very own treasured daughters.

Sacrificial love is the Father's pattern for the family. God is love. He is many other things as well, including righteous and just in all His ways, but He never acts apart from His love. As human beings, as His very own daughters, we were created in His image, created to be channels of His love. And if we truly belong to Him, this is possible because "the love of God has been poured out within our hearts through the Holy Spirit who was given to us" and "the fruit of the Spirit is love" (Romans 5:5; Galatians 5:22).

Every family needs a home. Not just a roof over their heads to keep them out of the rain, but a home prepared for life. Listen to what Jesus said in John 14:2: "In My Father's house are many dwelling places; if it were not so, I would have told you; for I go to prepare a place for you." God has a home—and it is prepared for His family! O precious daughter, do you realize God has called you to be the keeper of your family's earthly home until we're all reunited in heaven? What a magnificent privilege!

From Donna

I encourage you to study Titus 2:3-5 carefully. It reveals key life principles on being godly women, wives, mothers, and homemakers.

The High Calling of a Woman

God has prepared and keeps our eternal, heavenly home...and you, as a woman, have the high calling of preparing and keeping your family's earthly home. If you want to discover God's plan and pattern for your home, heed Paul's words to Titus:

Older women likewise are to be reverent in their behavior, not malicious gossips nor enslaved to much wine, teaching what is good, so that they may encourage the young women to love their husbands, to love their children, to be sensible, pure, workers at home, kind, being subject to their own husbands, so that the word of God will not be dishonored (Titus 2:3-5).

Note the words "young woman," and the words that follow. These are *God's words,* and this is *God's pattern.* Young women are to…

- love their husbands
- be sensible and pure
- be workers at home
- be subject to their husbands.

Do you see the words "workers at home"? The Greek term (the language the New Testament was originally written in) for "workers at home" is *oikourgous.* It comes from the word *oikeo,* or house, and that means you are to be a keeper of your house. In other words, this is your career, your unique calling from God. This is the pattern God gave us for the home and family.

He has called you to prepare a house like His house, a home like His home! A beautiful picture and foretaste of what is yet to come! And by doing this you bring pleasure to His heart and honor to His name. What a magnificent calling! And it's a calling from God Himself, the sovereign ruler of the universe.

A similar word to the Greek word for "workers at home" is also used in 1 Timothy, when Paul gives instructions regarding young widows in the church: "Therefore, I want younger widows to get married, bear children, keep house, and give the enemy no occasion for reproach; for some have already turned aside to follow Satan" (5:14-15).

Don't let "keep house" throw you. Our culture has so perverted and demeaned this precious way of serving that the term sometimes carries false baggage. The word used here is *oikodespoteo.* It means "to govern or manage a house or the domestic affairs of a family." You're a domestic engineer! According to this, dear lady, you are to be the master of the house; the home is your domain.

Men and Women in the Pattern

What then is the role of the husband? He's the provider. God makes this clear way back at the beginning, when He set the pattern in the Garden of Eden. He told Adam that a man was to labor six days a week. In 1 Timothy 5:8 Paul says that a man is to provide for his own—especially his own household. And if he doesn't, he's worse than an infidel.

In contrast, the primary role of the woman centers on family and home. The primary role of the man is *provider* for the family and home. That's the pattern for the home and family that God gave us—and nothing works better. When we live according to these precepts, beloved, we will find our greatest fulfillment as human beings. Why? Because no one knows a building better than its architect. And since God created men and women, invented marriage, and ordained the family, there's no one else who has more accurate information. He's the originator of the grand design, and the One who loved us so much He gave us a pattern for success in our homes and marriages.

From Emilie

At a Youniquely Woman Conference a single woman, whose mother lived with her, came up to me crying. She'd realized she was living in a "house" not a home. She had a small two-bedroom apartment...and didn't even have a table or chairs! The women in her group decided to help. On Friday evening, at our pj party, these sweet women surprised her with a table and two chairs. We all cried and were so blessed!

The Path of Life

A tragic news story came out of Oregon. A young California

family—a father, mother, and two young children—was trying to find a back road leading to the coast. Somehow, instead of turning onto a main highway, they turned onto a forest service road, got into an area covered with snow, and became lost. When their car got stuck, the young father set out on foot to get help. Instead of bringing help to his family, however, he became disoriented, then hopelessly lost, eventually dying of exposure in the wilderness. The rest of his family was finally rescued. Life will never be the same for them.

The true highway—the marked state highway—was a path of life for that young family. Along that established route were food, water, and shelter. Furthermore, it would have taken them where they wanted to go. And instead of enduring a heartbreaking tragedy, they might have enjoyed a memorable family vacation and gone on with their lives.

There is a path of life for each one of us as we walk with the Lord, keep in step with the Holy Spirit, and obey God's commands and precepts. Solomon wrote, "The way of life winds upward for the wise, that he may turn away from hell below" (Proverbs 15:24 NKJV). When we follow the pattern laid down in Scripture for us by our Creator, we escape many of the heartaches suffered by those who make their own patterns and go their own ways. But there's more to it than that! David said to the Lord, "You will make known to me the path of life; in Your presence is fullness of joy" (Psalm 16:11).

There is joy along the path of life! The psalmist said, "Make me walk in the path of Your commandments, *for I delight in it*" (Psalm 119:35). Following God's pattern for marriage and the family guides us away from destruction and brings us peace and sheer gladness of heart that no other way, no other pattern can bring. This isn't to say life will be perfect of course. We live in a fallen world. But remember, as children of God we are overcomers (1 John 4:4).

The Roles of Husband and Father

Part of the Great Architect's plan and pattern for the home involves making the husband the centerpiece. I realize this goes cross-grain to contemporary culture. But again, that's really nothing new. God's standards and priorities will always be mocked and belittled by those who reject Him and His Word.

As the Architect and Builder of all, God the Father is the centerpiece of heaven. He is the giver of good gifts, yet He also chastens and trains His children (Hebrews 11:10; 12:1-7). What does this mean, practically speaking? How is this pattern adapted here on earth? What I'm about to share sounds old fashioned and politically incorrect. Many would say these thoughts aren't worthy of the times in which we live, the place to which "we as women have arrived." Yet Scripture clearly teaches that we are to be in the world but not of it. We are not to be conformed to this world, but transformed by the renewing of our minds (John 17:14-23; Romans 12:1-2). The husband, not the children, is the centerpiece of the home, just as God the Father is the centerpiece of heaven.

Paul tells us in 1 Corinthians 11:7, "For a man ought not to have his head covered, since he is the image and glory of God; but the woman is the glory of man." What is "glory"? It's "the image, the expression of something." To glorify God is to give a correct opinion, a proper estimate of who He is. How does this play out in relationship to your husband?

When your husband comes home, what kind of welcome does he get? If you want to strengthen your marriage and your family and give everyone a great sense of security, begin by making your husband the center of your family life. What do I mean? Treat him like a king. Don't demean him, don't denigrate him, and don't try to dethrone him. When he comes through the front door in the evening after work, you should look good, smell good, and greet him with a kiss. If dinner isn't ready yet, sauté a few onions so the delicious smell gives assurance that food is coming. Don't bombard him with problems or complaints or honey-do's as soon as he steps through the door.

Remember where your husband has just come from, what he's been doing, and the responsibilities that lie on his shoulders. Let him know you're glad to see him and grant him a little time to peacefully unwind.

Yes, I know...you've been working all day too. One of the kids gave you a hard time, the laundry is stacked up, the cupboard may be a little bare, and you feel like you're stuck between those four walls. But this is life!

When the time is right, you can share your concerns and disappointments with your husband. But not when he first walks through the door! The fact is, dear one, marriage and home life may not be the ideal you want or that you dreamed of. There are long, tedious stretches on the road of life. But marriage is still a good route heading toward a very good destination. You may not like the scenery right now, but you will like where the road takes you. Commit your cares and burdens to the Lord, and watch Him work! You will have your heavenly Father's blessing because you're a loyal and obedient daughter. If you'll follow God's pattern, you'll have no regrets.

> *The wise woman builds her house, but*
> *the foolish tears it down with her own hands.*
>
> PROVERBS 14:1

Bringing a Little Heaven into Your Home

As we saw earlier, our heavenly home is a prepared and beautiful place. Preparing a home in such a way—making it beautiful in your eyes and in the eyes of your family—takes time, energy, ingenuity, and creativity. You may say, "But, Kay, my home is so small. It's just an apartment with the two (or however many) of us. We don't have much except each other right now."

The truth is, it doesn't really matter how small your dwelling is or how tight your budget happens to be. That doesn't diminish the importance of your role at all! As the manager and keeper, you can make sure your home is a place of order, peace, and pleasantness.

Think about it. God has given you the responsibility and privilege of creating an island of beauty and tranquility in the midst of a careless, increasingly hostile world. That's a wonderful thought to ponder, but establishing this type of household won't happen by wishing and wanting. You need to work toward that end by living intentionally. Plan. Organize. Delegate. As an added bonus, this helps train your children for their roles in life.

The Proverbs 31 Woman

As noted, God gives us patterns for living in His Word, and because He is the Architect and Designer of men, women, and marriage, He knows what will bring the most sweetness and peace into our lives. One such pattern can be found in Proverbs 31. In this chapter the writer describes "an excellent wife." *Excellent* is the Hebrew word *hayil,* which means "of strong moral fiber." As you read through the chapter, it becomes glaringly apparent that society's values are so different today. I don't often do this in my Bible studies but this Proverbs 31 woman can be described in eight words that begin with the letter "D." Let's consider her qualities together.

> *Devotion:* "The heart of her husband trusts in her, and he will have no lack of gain. She does him good and not evil all the days of her life" (Proverbs 31:11-12).
>
> *Duty:* "She looks for wool and flax and works with her hands in delight. She is like merchant ships; she brings her food from afar" (verses 13-14).
>
> *Discipline:* "She rises also while it is still night and gives food to her household and portions to her maidens" (verse 15).
>
> *Discernment:* "She considers a field and buys it; from her earnings she plants a vineyard" (verse 16).
>
> *Direction:* "She girds herself with strength and makes her arms strong. She senses that her gain is good; her lamp does not go out at night. She stretches out her hands to the distaff, and her hands grasp the spindle. She extends her hand to the poor, and she stretches out her hands to the needy" (verses 17-20).

Decorum: "She is not afraid of the snow for her household, for all her household are clothed with scarlet. She makes coverings for herself; her clothing is fine linen and purple. Her husband is known in the gates, when he sits among the elders of the land. She makes linen garments and sells them, and supplies belts to the tradesmen. Strength and dignity are her clothing, and she smiles at the future" (verses 21-25).

Discretion: "She opens her mouth in wisdom, and the teaching of kindness is on her tongue. She looks well to the ways of her household, and does not eat the bread of idleness. Her children rise up and bless her; her husband also, and he praises her, saying: 'Many daughters have done nobly, but you excel them all'" (verses 26-29).

Dedication: "Charm is deceitful and beauty is vain, but a woman who fears the LORD, she shall be praised. Give her the product of her hands, and let her works praise her in the gates" (verses 30-31).

A Haven of Righteousness

Just as heaven is a prepared place and a place of beauty, it is also a place of righteousness. When speaking of the new heavens and new earth, Peter speaks of a place "in which righteousness dwells" (2 Peter 3:13). The apostle John, speaking of the New Jerusalem that will someday come down out of heaven to the earth—glistening and flashing like a great jewel lit from within—tells us that "nothing unclean, and no one who practices abomination and lying, shall ever come into it" (Revelation 21:27).

This should be our goal, daughters. Our homes should be havens of righteousness, and every member of the family needs to understand this. I remember Anna Hayford (Jack Hayford's wife) sharing with me that when her children wanted to do something that was culturally correct but fell short of God's standards of righteousness, she told them, "We're Hayfords, and we don't do that." Insert your own family name in that sentence. Your children need to remember and say, "We're the _____. We belong to God, and we don't do those things." One of God's names is *Jehovah Tsidkenu*—"the Lord our Righteousness." And since we are His children and derive our name from Him, that's the way we need to live. How I wish I'd taught this to my children when they were young!

As I was cleaning up my office one night, I had a history documentary playing on TV. The host of the program was interviewing an elderly Japanese man who had been a pilot during the surprise attack on the United States naval fleet in Pearl Harbor. He recalled that before that attack their military commanders told them they were to give their lives for the sake of Japan—even if their planes were shot down in flames and they became as charred crusts.

And what was his response? Excitement and anticipation. He said, "The words stirred my soul to think that I had this high honor to do for my country. I was eager to get my plane in the air!" This loyal citizen lived for a higher purpose. We need to do the same, knowing that ours is an eternal purpose, a righteous purpose. Someday Jesus will reign over earth and the universe in beautiful, radiant righteousness, brighter than the brightest of His stars. As women of God, you and I are called to prepare our homes and our families today for that beginning!

What television programs get watched in your home? Do your children know when to turn the channel? What their eyes shouldn't look at? I know children who have thrown their little hands over their eyes and called Mommy to come and "fix the television" when confronted with inappropriate images. Recently my teenage grandson and I were watching a DVD drama about World War II when a totally unnecessary sex scene flashed across the screen. I hadn't realized this movie had such content and was totally flustered. My grandson, however, simply closed his eyes until it was over. It was an automatic response because that is how he's been trained.

That is righteousness. That's part of creating a safe, joyful, God-honoring atmosphere and environment under your roof.

What kind of magazines, catalogs, books, and DVDs are in your home? What access is permitted on the Internet, how long do your children spend surfing the Web, and how well is that time monitored? Yes, keeping tabs on such things can be a difficult, time-consuming task. It would be much easier to simply "let it go," and not guard against such things.

But what if you knew you had a mold problem in your basement? Would you ignore it? Pretend it wasn't there even though you knew that day by day it was eroding the value of your house and the health of your family? No, of course not. You would take immediate steps to deal with it. How much more important to guard our homes and families against the moral decay and corrosion of popular culture!

From Donna

According to the Bureau of Labor statistics, the jobs of home and childcare are worth over $139,000 a year in today's economy.

What is the conversation like around your dinner table or in the family room? How are people talked about and described? Do you have standards about what is permissible to say? The earlier you establish boundaries, the easier they will be to uphold as your children mature.

We can all look back on major events or milestones in our lives: graduation from high school or college, marriage, moving days, children coming into the world. These tend to stand out, but life is mostly lived *between* those big and memorable events. The fabric of life really consists of our approach and our commitment to living each day in a certain way, following a certain pattern. Living *intentionally.*

Discuss with your husband what you'd like your home atmosphere to be and set the parameters for your children. Write them out, and then post them, teach them, and uphold them. Though it requires thought and effort from both of you and the courage to stand by your convictions, you will never, never regret it.

A Place of Peace

Heaven is a place of peace, where all tears will be wiped away. There will be no more mourning, crying, or pain (Revelation 21:3-4). Is your home "a little bit of heaven" when it comes to peace? A place where your family feels loved, safe, and secure? Or is it filled with bickering, screaming, hateful words, put-downs, and pain? Some of the most hurtful words ever spoken have been spoken among family members under the roof of their own home, in a place God intended to be a refuge from the harsh, hostile world.

You, dear daughter, are the thermostat of the home. It's true! You and your husband are the parents, and as such you set and enforce the standards, the parameters of acceptable behavior. Children need discipline—and want it! They need restraints on their tempers, their tongues, their tantrums. I've worked with teens for more than 30 years, and I've heard this confirmed over and over. I hear, "I wish my parents had been more strict" and "I wish my parents cared enough about me to want to know where I was and told me when I had to be home."

All of us are happier with some structure and boundaries in our lives—and children are no exception, no matter how they might grouse about it. Think of a river pouring through a broken dike, churning up mud, weeds, tree limbs, and trash and bringing destruction as it sweeps across a landscape. Now think of that same powerful river safely within its banks, a thing of beauty, productivity, life, traveling with purpose and definition as it moves toward the sea.

Structure, rules, expectations, and discipline—in a life, in a family, in a home—produce "a harvest of righteousness and peace for those who have been trained by it" (Hebrews 12:11 NIV).

A Place of Joy

Heaven is also a place of overflowing joy. In Psalm 16:11 David writes, "You will make known to me the path of life; in Your presence is fullness of joy; in Your right hand there are pleasures forever." Is it fun to be in your home? Is home a place of smiles, joy, genuine pleasure, enjoyment, and encouragement? Is there laughter in the walls? I believe that the very atmosphere of heaven—the celestial air that we'll breathe in the Lord's presence—will be full of joy. Homes have an atmosphere too…and I'm not talking about pollen or dust mites. You can usually sense the atmosphere of a home the minute you walk through the door. If the joy of the Lord's presence and the echoes of family fun are present under your roof, those who enter will experience a sense of lightness and welcome. It will be a relaxing, enjoyable place to be.

Dear daughter, all of this starts with you. Are you content with where God has placed you? Are you fun to be with? Is there lightness and joy in your heart? Do you know laughing is good for the body? It's true! A good, long laugh releases happy, feel-good hormones. To me there's nothing harder than living with a grouch…or a pessimist…or a cynic. So I want to be a fun person to be around. I want to feel free to laugh, kid, joke, and play. I certainly don't want to become a stodgy, grumpy, talking-about-my-ills old woman.

I think our most fun times as a family were around the dinner table. I well remember when it was just Jack, our three sons, and the only two females in the house—me and Ebony, our little black poodle. Nobody ever told Ebony she was just a poodle, so she assumed she was part of the family and went just about everywhere we went. I can also close my eyes right now and see family scenes of us all crowded around the table on a porch we made into a beautiful, light-filled dining room. Now the delightful crowd includes four grandsons and five granddaughters! As our sons rehearse their antics as children growing up on the 32-acre campus of Precepts Ministries, we laugh until tears flow.

Beloved, your home can be your ministry. Make it a magnet for others—especially your children's friends. If they are in your home enjoying your island of peace and joy, you can be a beautiful advertisement for the kingdom of heaven. Give visitors a taste of heaven on earth!

Heaven Is a Place of Abundant Entrance

There is an abundant entrance waiting for us when we approach heaven's front door. We will experience a welcome beyond anything we can ever imagine. "Be all the more diligent to make certain about His calling and choosing you; for as long as you practice these things, you will never stumble; for in this way the entrance into the eternal kingdom [heaven] of our Lord and Savior Jesus Christ will be abundantly supplied to you" (2 Peter 1:10-11).

What is the "entrance" like for your husband and children when they walk into your house? Is no one at home? Is the house dark and empty? No cookies, no milk, no one to talk to them about their day? Maybe a note stuck on the fridge with a phone number in case they need to call? Who's there to hug them and say, "I'm so glad you're home"?

From Emilie

Play "Pick-up" with your young kids. Before meals or bedtime help your children pick up clothes, toys, books, and loose items and put them away. Be enthusiastic and make it fun!

Thomas Kinkade, the world-renowned artist who paints scenes of beauty and tranquility, often speaks about his childhood, about coming home after school to a dark, cheerless house through a weed-infested front yard. When his father left the family, Thomas' mother became the breadwinner and was always at work when the two boys came home at night. Because of that memory of a dark, unattractive house, Thomas fills the homes in his paintings with warm, radiant, inviting light...and smoke curling from the chimney. When you look at his paintings, you always see homes with every window lighted in welcome.

Here's a disturbing picture. Imagine stepping into heaven and hearing an argument. Yelling and screaming echoing through the air. Can you envision arriving and finding the lights out and no one to greet you? Or perhaps someone who does greet you—with a list of jobs to do now that you're finally home? Or perhaps someone chewing you out for one reason or another the minute you step through the veil and into your forever home? Or how about this? What if you walked into heaven and saw junk lying around on dusty streets of gold? What if you entered a celestial mansion and saw dirty dishes filling the sink, heavenly robes thrown here and there, and garbage overflowing the trash cans?

"Well," you say, "I can't imagine such a thing. That wouldn't be heaven." And you're right! And neither will your home be a little slice of heaven on earth if it looks trashed when your family walks through the door. I encourage you to take a fresh look around. Are there areas that need to be more organized? Cleaned? Straightened? Does anything need replaced or updated? Dear daughter of the King, do all you can to bring a little heaven to earth for your family.

May I recommend a wonderful book on home and family? *The Home Experience* by Devi Titus and Marilyn Weiher shares practical ways to help you make your home a sanctuary, a peaceful haven for your family.[1]

A Spirit of Welcome

Emilie

Welcome home!

That's what I want my life to say to everyone whose path crosses mine. I want to create an atmosphere of serenity and joy, blessing and belonging that embraces people and draws them in. I want them to feel loved, special, and cared for. Kay calls it creating "a little bit of heaven."

I'll never forget my excitement more than 52 years ago when my husband, Bob, carried me over the threshold of our first apartment. It had three tiny rooms, but it felt like a castle. Bob was a first-year teacher, fresh from college. I was a 17-year-old bride still in my last year of high school and working for my mama in her little dress shop. Bob and I were so proud of our very first home, and we put our hearts and souls into making it a comfortable and inviting place.

Together we sprayed white paint on the old wrought-iron lawn table someone gave us, creating a dainty but sturdy dining table. I sewed pink eyelet curtains for the windows while Bob spray painted egg cartons to glue on the walls for a "white-on-white" texture. We had one canvas chair, a box for a lamp table, and an old trunk for a coffee table. We found great joy living there together and sharing our apartment with others.

It was many years later—after our children left the nest and a progression of condos and tract homes—that we finally crossed the threshold of the converted barn that became our home for many years. We saw such potential in that lovely old house—the hardwood floors, the high-ceilinged great room, the kitchen with its dozens of cupboards and cabinets, and the tree-covered grounds. We had so much fun remodeling and redecorating and landscaping to make it ours.

What we did in our dream house was really no different from what we'd done in that little apartment years before. And it was no different from what you do in your house, apartment, or condominium.

The Art of Homemaking

What were Bob and I doing? We were homemaking—literally "making a home." We were creating a lifestyle that said "welcome" to ourselves and to everyone around us. Henry Van Dyke spun this sweet little poem:

> *Every house where love abides*
> *And friendship is a guest*
> *Is surely home and home, sweet home*
> *For there the heart can rest.*

What Kay wrote earlier in this chapter is so true. We should never minimize the value and meaning of "home as a refuge" in a hostile world and an increasingly godless culture. Why is a "welcome home" lifestyle so important? I truly believe we all need a spiritual center, a place where we belong. A place where we can unwind, regroup, and get back in touch with who we truly are…and then reach out to share that refuge with others.

Viewed in this way "welcome home" doesn't necessarily mean a physical location. Home is as much a state of the heart and spirit as it is a specific place. Many a person living on the road has learned to make herself at home in hotel rooms, other people's houses, or wherever she finds herself.

And yet…just as our spirits require physical bodies to do God's work here on earth, most of us need a physical location we can go to and call ours. And we have the privilege of making the place where we live a welcoming refuge for ourselves and others—a place where the spirit of loveliness can find a foothold in our lives.

"Well," you say, "I don't have time to spend on a project like that—and I certainly don't have the money." Actually, it doesn't have to cost much of either.

Cultivating an "I Can" Attitude

I've seen "welcome home" living spaces created by stay-at-home moms, high-priced executives, and a just-graduated bachelor or two. It doesn't require a professional's touch in decorating, elaborate meal preparation, or extensive handyman skills. What it *does* require is a caring, willing spirit—a determination to think beyond bare-bones necessities and to make room in our lives, schedules, and budgets for what pleases the senses and enriches the soul. No, I'm not talking about a degree in interior decorating or a large home-furnishings budget. I'm simply saying that a positive "I can do it" attitude will take you a long way. Many of us just need to gain confidence that we have something to share and the ability to do it.

That special sense of "I can" is what I hope you find in this book—along with some simple, practical ideas for making "welcome home" a way of life. As you read through our suggestions and insights, I hope the spirit of loveliness that lives within you is touched, motivating you to make changes that will further the spirit of welcome in your life.

From Kay

When I didn't have money for vases or flowers, I learned all sorts of things can be used: pretty bottles, small pitchers, creamers and sugar bowls—anything that can hold water. A jar with raffia or a ribbon tied around it. And what did I put in them? Wild daisies and branches from bushes, shrubs, and trees. It's amazing what a single flower or a touch of green does to a room.

A Safe Refuge

"God is our refuge and strength, a very present help in trouble. Therefore we will not fear, though the earth should change and though the mountains slip into the heart of the sea; though its waters roar and foam, though the mountains quake at its swelling pride" (Psalm 46:1-3). God is a refuge in times of trouble, tumult, and turmoil. "When the ground starts shifting under my feet," the psalmist is saying, "when my world becomes a worrisome, fearful place, I take refuge in my God."

God is a refuge for His people. He always has been, and He always will be. And I believe that a godly home—a home where Jesus Christ is obeyed and honored—becomes a physical refuge, a place where people worn down by the noise, commotion, and hostility of the outside world can find a safe resting place. A welcoming home is a place you and others enjoy coming to.

From Donna

Remember to have the welcome mat out first and foremost— and with the most care and attention— for your husband and children.

If you live in a house with small children, you may already be shaking your head. "What do you mean, 'noise, commotion, and hostility of the outside world'? I have to *leave* home to get away from the turmoil!" Believe me, I understand. But even in the rough-and-tumble of family living, home can be a safe haven and even a place of quiet (at least some of the time). If you find noise and activity crowding your family life and pushing and pulling at you, making the extra effort to create a sense of refuge in the midst of it can pay wonderful dividends.

Maybe this concept depends on how you define "refuge." I'm not talking about a hole you disappear down to eat and sleep and then emerge to go about the business of life. A welcoming home is where real life happens. It's where personalities are nurtured, growth is stimulated, and people feel free to be and improve themselves. That caring, nurturing quality—not the absence of noise or occasional strife—is what makes a home a refuge.

Creating this kind of environment may require special efforts from single people. If you live alone, it's easy to fall into the "hole" mentality and deprive yourself of the spiritual and emotional benefits of a welcoming home. Writer Andrea Wells Miller learned the value of such a home during her single days when she came home from a business trip to her empty apartment:

> As I looked around, only my ivy plant looked back. The pillows on the sofa, the bedroom slippers out of place and askew on the floor, the dusty end table with a dirty coffee cup on it, all reminded me that I was alone. No one had bothered anything while I was away. Everything was just as I had left it.
>
> I went the short distance from the entry hall into the kitchen. Everything was neat and clean, except the coffee percolator sitting alone on the cabinet...I opened the lid and looked inside—green moldy splotches were floating on the half inch of coffee I had not poured out. It amazed me how quickly mold could grow.

And so Andrea learned to counteract that "empty apartment" feeling by making a few simple changes. She plugged her lamp and radio into a wall socket connected to the light switch by the door. That way one flip of a switch produced lights and music. She also made a point, when possible, of cleaning up ahead of time, leaving fresh towels, fresh sheets, and a clean coffeepot. "Those little changes," she writes, "helped me feel warm and welcomed when I returned from a trip."

As Andrea discovered, it doesn't take much to make a home feel like a delightful haven. Soft light—lamps, candlelight, even firelight—rather than harsh overhead glare. Soothing music. Something bright or pretty near the door to greet visitors and people coming home. Pleasant fragrances: scented candles, potpourri, spices boiling on the stove, or—most powerful of all—dinner in the oven. Taking just five minutes to straighten the vestibule and light a welcoming candle can make a huge contribution to presenting a welcoming sanctuary for anyone who steps inside.

A Sense of Order

A welcoming home portrays a sense of order. I'm not talking about having a stiff, stultifying attitude that goes to pieces over a speck of dust or that sacrifices relationships in the interest of cleanliness. I'm talking about cultivating a comforting, confident sense that life is under control. A sense that people—not possessions—are in charge of the household. That emotions may be expressed but never used as weapons; that life is proceeding with purpose according to an overall plan.

A welcoming home is organized around making life easier and more meaningful. Its physical tidiness frees us to enjoy the beauty in our surroundings and concern ourselves with more important matters than unearthing a clean shirt or battling an invasion of roaches. And yes, I am talking about cleaning house. But I'm also talking about goal setting, time management, and family negotiations—but not as ends in themselves. In a truly welcoming home, organization takes its proper place in the overall scheme of the universe. The daily chores of maintenance become something we can glory in, partly because they don't overwhelm us or define our existence.

Most of us respond positively to this kind of order in our lives. And there is a reason for that. We are made in the image of God, and God organized the whole universe to proceed in a measured, orderly fashion. Think of creation. God brought a beautiful, populated globe out of darkness and chaos. He is the ultimate organizer, and the results of His ordering spirit are always good. Concerning the worship of the Corinthian church, Paul wrote, "All things must be done properly and in an orderly manner" (1 Corinthians 14:40). It's the same with our home environment; we automatically feel more comfortable and welcome when we sense God's touch and order in our lives.

But don't let this talk of order and organization make you feel guilty or panicked. Even if chaos and clutter in your home and life are wearing you down, the solution is not a frenetic, whirlwind effort to "get organized." Unless you begin with your heart, the most complete reorganization of house and home will simply give you a clean slate for future chaos. And it may also drive you and everyone else crazy in the process.

Humans weren't made to "get organized." We were made to live as God's children, worshiping Him and delighting in Him. As we open our hearts and attitudes to God, putting Him first in our lives and looking to Him for guidance, He will show us little ways to organize the chaos and achieve a more peaceful, ordered existence. In another context, the apostle Paul wrote: "God wants his children to live in peace" (1 Corinthians 7:15 TLB).

All these changes don't have to happen at once. Growing in the spirit of loveliness is a lifelong, step-by-step process of discovery. It's taken me 37 years to develop the systems that help me maintain order and a sense of welcome in my life and home—and I'm still learning. And I'm pleased I can share with you what I've learned to help you create a sense of comforting order and welcoming loveliness in your home.

Three

Modeling a
Balanced Life

7 Subtle Time Traps

Donna

Most moms I talk to think the idea of a balanced life is just an idealized dream—a goal as unattainable as jumping the Grand Canyon or swimming the Pacific Ocean. A balanced life, however, is just abundant life in bite-sized pieces. And the Lord Jesus promised us "life more abundant" (John 10:10). Emilie, Kay, and I are here to tell you that *a balanced life can be accomplished...and it's worth working for!* I've learned quite a bit about this process of balancing the demands of life, and I'm hoping you'll let me mentor you with a bit of "older woman" wisdom.

Detour to the Seventh Floor

Picture the following scene: I'm all dressed up—suit and high heels...and looking good, if I don't say so myself. I'm attending a huge conference. I am the keynote speaker. My picture is plastered everywhere—in the elevators, on the registration tables, and on prominent signs leading into the banquet hall. Naturally everyone assumes that *the* speaker has her life "all together" and knows how to bring the insights for doing so gift-wrapped for the assembled ladies.

Stepping into the elevator I get smiles and nods of recognition. They've seen my pictures on the posters. I nod in return and engage in polite conversation. Inevitably someone asks, "Aren't you *the* speaker—Donna Otto?"

"I am," I reply, feeling cool. (I've always wanted to be cool.)

The elevator stops. I smile graciously at those inside, and step out into the hallway, ready to walk through the lobby. Only…it isn't the lobby. It's the seventh floor, and I've made my exit prematurely.

Now what? My options are limited. I can say, "Oops!" and step back into the elevator (losing my "class" and negating my "cool factor"), or I can pretend I planned all along to exit on the seventh floor, wait for the next elevator, and proceed. Either way I'm busted.

Life is like this every day, whether we're in a hotel or not. At various times in our lives, each of us is the featured person in an event, a family, or a group. And sometimes it's hard to get off at the right floor. Most of the time, in fact, we end up publicly or privately on the wrong floor, a place other than where God wants us to be. And it's usually a matter of mismanagement and not paying attention. Doors open and we assume we should walk through them. But sometimes we should and sometimes we shouldn't. Open doors represent new challenges, which can be good or time traps that keep us from God's purposes—the seventh floors of life.

Balance, however, demands you make a choice, and there is usually a right choice to make. I made the right choice that day on the elevator. To the delight of my fellow elevator passengers, I stepped out, did a double-take, said, "Yikes! Wait for me!" and hurried back in. Usually the return to balance isn't always that easy or that immediate. Balance begins with saying yes to the key things in life and no to the enticement of the seventh floor.

Enough Hours

You might argue that there isn't enough time to live a balanced life, that there aren't enough hours in a day to fit in everything good. In answer to that, I want to share 12 words that may be the most significant, life-changing words ever spoken to me outside of the Bible. These words, if you adopt them, will help you make wise choices.

And choices matter. They are the key to a life pleasing to God. Here is the statement:

There are enough hours every day to do the will of God.

Coming at it from another angle, Jesus said much the same thing. Listen to Matthew 6:32-34 in this wonderful paraphrase:

> People who don't know God and the way he works fuss over these things, but you know both God and how he works. Steep your life in God-reality, God-initiative, God-provisions. Don't worry about missing out. You'll find all your everyday human concerns will be met.

> Give your entire attention to what God is doing right now, and don't get worked up about what may or may not happen tomorrow. God will help you deal with whatever hard things come up when the time comes (Matthew 6:32-34 MSG).

That, dear daughters in the Lord, is the way to live in balance. Believe me, I know. I've tried other ways and failed. Thirty-plus years ago I was faced daily with these humiliating situations and circumstances:

- lost car keys (3 times a day)
- negative mail
- unpaid bills
- unfinished projects
- unanswered correspondence
- an expired driver's license
- dirty dishes hidden in dryer
- strained relationships
- image management issues (time, money, and energy spent on maintaining an image—to look good to others)

To be honest, these daily situations were spiraling out of control.

I missed a very significant event, and my absence was conspicuous and noted. (I forgot to write it on my calendar.) I couldn't find an important document when I needed it (because I had piles of paper stuffed everywhere). And to top everything off, I was facing a furious friend (because I forgot her and didn't see what the big deal was). All of these things and more combined to make me see that, in a word, I was *undone*.

At this point I could have stepped off on the "seventh floor," giving myself over to discouragement and despair. Instead I stayed on board until I found the right place—and that was in God's Word. If you've ever met me in person, among the first facts you discovered about me was I ask questions—lots of questions. And I want you to know that I've never asked a question I didn't find the answer to in the Bible. Reading the Bible also raises questions—better, deeper questions—in my heart. As I read and meditate, the Holy Spirit stimulates my thinking and begins to quietly rearrange me...bringing me back into sweet balance.

So in my undone state I went to God's Word in desperation, prayerfully seeking help. The first phase of help came from a surprising source. It was an insight arising out of the Lord's Prayer—perhaps the most prayed, memorized, and recited prayer in the world. You know it...

> Our Father in heaven, hallowed be your name.
> Your kingdom come, your will be done,
>   on earth as it is in heaven.
> Give us this day our daily bread, and forgive us our debts,
>   as we also have forgiven our debtors.
> And lead us not into temptation, but deliver us from evil
> (Matthew 6:9-13).

In the midst of this wonderful prayer, I found my first course of direction. *His will, not mine. His daily to-do list, not mine. His priorities, not mine.* The bottom line? I took a deep breath and started looking for a different perspective in life—for God's perspective. As I did, realization dawned on me. I'd been making lists for the sake of making lists.

The lists had become more important to me than the tasks. Sometimes I would accomplish a task that wasn't on my list—and then write it down after the fact so I could cross it off! But these were *my* lists, *my* priorities, and *my* attempts at ordering my life. I asked God for His list and His order. In the early stages of the changes, God helped me see that my time was not mine and not about me. My time belonged to Him, and it was His agenda that counted.

From Emilie

Have you ever forgotten to return something you borrowed? Select a shelf or basket and label it "Items Borrowed." Use it! You'll know where items are and when to return them.

Because of my book topics, I'm often asked to speak at conferences and retreats on organization and order. From time to time my host will mention "time management" as my topic. After years of careful thought, I've concluded that no one can manage time. At best we can manage ourselves. Each of us has the same number of hours in every week—no more, no less. If you are at all (even in the smallest degree) like me, you'll agree that managing yourself is not easy. I've found that I can be unruly and unpredictable, frequently exiting at the sixth or seventh floors instead of staying on course for where I need to be.

Frankly, I'd rather manage you than me.

But self-management is key to submitting to God's will...rather than blindly following your own. Living in the twenty-first century means being on the lookout for traps set to pull you away from God's priorities. Being forewarned about potential traps will help you stay on task...on His ways and His list. Do you know the snares that distract you and rob you of time? Here are a few that come to mind.

No Priorities Established

The word *priority* comes from *prior,* meaning before. In setting priorities, consider what has come before. A challenge I regularly deal with is not pausing to assess my prior commitments, especially the lifelong ones, when asked to do something. We need to make sure new and "urgent" priorities don't compel us to abandon our most important and basic priorities.

Here is a good example. My only daughter met her husband-to-be, planned a large wedding, married, moved to Michigan, and had two children in less than five years. *(Wow!)* Needless to say, during this time my daughter's choices had a huge impact on me and my choices. The principles of "love the Lord your God" and "love others" are my underlying values—and Anissa's choices reinforced those in my heart.

Loving God as He directed was easy. Encouraging my daughter in each new stage was easy. Admiring Jason, my son-in-law, was easy. Meeting and falling in love with Samuel, my first grandchild, was more than easy, as was the case with my granddaughter, Elliana. All of these things were easy, easy, easy.

What was *not* easy was rearranging my goals, plans, calendar, and work to have the time to love these new "others" in my life. Every time Anissa—a precious commitment of mine—said yes, my life was altered.

We all need to make room in our hearts and lives for the expansion of our original and lifelong priorities, even at the expense of newer and, supposedly, more "urgent" ones.

Too Much Technology

Writer Dan Sullivan suggests that being connected to various forms of technology "24/7–365" can be a hidden and costly time trap.[1] While we certainly don't want to return to Pony Express days, adapting to anything and everything offered can subtly rob you of energy to manage your life. For instance, when the latest technology gadget is coming to stores people line up for days to be the first to get one. Dear daughters, let there be limits. If we chase after every new piece of technology, we end up letting people who don't really know us or care about us set our priorities.

In his book *Social Intelligence,* Daniel Goleman concludes that, as human beings, we are wired to connect. He writes:

Long before the iPod, the Walkman, and the cell phone cauterized people walking down the street, blocking off raw contact with the bustle of life, the auto—a mode of passing through a public space utterly insulated by wraparound glass, a half-ton or more of steel, and the lulling sound of the radio—started the process. Before the auto became commonplace, typical modes of travel—from walking or being pulled along by a horse to riding a bullock-cart—kept travelers in easy proximity to the human world around them.[2]

A number of years ago my husband, David, suggested we get a fax machine. I resisted. He insisted. Finally I agreed. Within the first month of ownership, we were awakened twice in the middle of the night by the shrill ringing of our new must-have machine. And for what? Junk mail! In software programs designed to market various products, phone numbers are sequenced and called automatically. And we were at the mercy of the marketers. We quickly changed how we used the fax—turning it on only when *we* want to receive or send.

Ah, but fax machines are almost ancient history now. "Personal" technology has exploded. We have cell phones, pagers, iPods, e-mail, iPhones, Blackberries, Blueberries, text messaging, CDs, DVDs, MP3s, HDTV, satellite radio, video games. And the list goes on and on…and will forever probably. The bottom line for each of these devices is that if you turn it on, it commands your attention.

Yes, I realize the help these new innovations bring, and I do use some of them. But here's the key…*some* of them. I encourage you to choose your technological tools carefully or you'll find the tools using you and taking all your time.

Exposure to Disconnected Information

Shortly after the turn of the twenty-first century an advertising agency noted that Americans were exposed to a minimum of 3000 advertising hits daily. After I finished wincing, I insisted this statistic had to be wrong. It sounded impossible. In the end, however, I was convinced. An advertising "hit" includes anything that passes before our conscious or subconscious mind, including bulletins, coupons, flyers, TV and radio commercials, newspaper and magazine ads, billboards and signage, and those annoying pop-up ads on websites.

Look around you. Is there a label showing on your shoes, purse, shirt, jeans, T-shirt, coffee cup, water bottle? You've just been hit! All these advertising hits and information from technology sources combine to occupy our minds with trivial matters. And it's the world's list of priorities, not yours…and certainly not God's. John had something to say about believers getting wrapped up in the world's chatter:

> Do not love the world or the things in the world. If anyone loves the world, the love of the Father is not in him. For all that is in the world—the desires of the flesh and the desires of the eyes and pride in possessions—is not from the Father but is from the world. And the world is passing away along with its desires, but whoever does the will of God abides forever (1 John 2:15-17).

What do we do about this? As I advised earlier, limiting exposure to TV and radio is a start. We get into the habit of having noise around us all day, never realizing how the advertising messages are being drilled into our memories. Then, when we find ourselves in a moment of quiet, we feel edgy and want to flip a switch to resume the noise.

Make friends with silence. Carry around a verse or two of Scripture on a three-by-five card so you can meditate on eternal truths during those rare unoccupied minutes in your day. Listen for the Lord's still, small voice speaking to your spirit. He may have been trying to get your attention for a long time.

Ideals and Values Trivialized

We live in a culture that, to a greater and greater degree, despises and rejects biblical and traditional values. In the Niagara Falls of information that deluges us daily, some of the most precious and important values and ideals of our lives are swept aside or at least marginalized. Keeping our godly and vital lifetime principles at the forefront of our thinking, where they should be, can be exhausting. In every conversation or message communicating the world's values, we need to be on guard. So often in the course of my day I find myself preparing my heart for yet another onslaught against what I believe in and hold dear.

Today's world solves problems with information and knowledge, not necessarily wisdom. Living in the midst of such an environment can create a profound sense of loss and confusion. When the name of Jesus is made a subject of jest; when sitcoms poke holes in core values such as honesty, kindness, marriage, gender roles; and when material consumption is the highest ideal, real values and ideals are trivialized. Time and energy are lost as we counteract that propaganda mentally, spiritually, and physically.

A Multiplying Array of Choices

A few years ago I pulled into the parking lot at my husband's favorite home-away-from-home, Home Depot. My mission that day was simple and straightforward: I needed to replace two of our toilet seats. Do you know there is an entire toilet seat aisle in that store? I discovered 84 choices! How could there possibly be that many variations on the basic model?

This started me thinking, and when I went to the grocery store later that day I counted 102 options for loaves of bread and 119 varieties of dry cereal. How long do you want to spend choosing items in these categories? How many nutrition labels do you want to read? Choices take time—time we often can't afford to waste.

Dependence on Inefficient Bureaucracy

In a poll I recently conducted among 500 women, I found that 100 percent of them hated automated telephone menus. You know what I'm talking about. You dial a number trying to get a little information or feedback, and you get connected to an automated machine telling you to push one for English, two for Spanish, and then you encounter another menu! One for the status of your account, two, three, and four for something else. Push the wrong button and you have to start over!

These systems save money for the organizations that use them, but you and I pay the price in decreased efficiency and increased time on the phone. Nine times out of 10, we have to "stay on the line for an available service representative" anyway.

This time trap causes anxiety and chaos, robbing you of calm and peace. Dealing with poorly managed or people-unfriendly companies robs you of time. In many cases you won't have any other options, but being prepared for these delays will help you better manage your life.

The Pace of Today

A friend of mine shared an interesting quote from her pastor: "The greatest barrier to community in the twenty-first century is the pace of life...You cannot rejoice with those who rejoice or weep with those who weep in a hurry." I thought of that quote recently as I watched my two-year-old grandson consume a carton of strawberry yogurt. He and his family were supposed to leave for church in less than an hour. He was not dressed, had not finished eating, and didn't have his "stuff" ready to go. He was simply eating his yogurt. One...bite... at...a...time.

Yes, getting ready for church was important, and there were certain tasks that had to be done. But my grandson reminded me that some things are meant to be savored. It takes time to enjoy the nearness of God and to hear His voice. It takes time to savor His beautiful creation, noticing and appreciating His many creative details.

The fact is, we can't enjoy much of anything if we're always rushing. Just as we can't deepen our relationships with one another on the fly, we can't deepen our relationship with God on the run. There are seasons (parenting an infant) and days (when our available time before 9:00 AM gets eaten up by "issues") that spending time with our heavenly Father happens behind the steering wheel. But this can't be sustained as a pattern for high quality of life.

After a nerve-jangling experience of crowds, demands, and little time to think or speak to one another, Jesus said to His men, "Come away by yourselves to a secluded place and rest a while" (Mark 6:31 NASB). This applies to you and me too! Elisabeth Elliot, my mentor and a hero of the faith, told me many times, "God will always give you everything you need to do His will, including time. Don't live in a rush."

Beyond these seven specific traps, you may encounter any of the following: unrelenting noise, information overload, and decreased face-to-face relational opportunities (sometimes referred to as "social corrosion"). How do we deal with time-stealing traps that throw us off balance and rob us of effectiveness and joy? Ask God for His plan...and be ready for anything!

Make a Plan

Many years ago a very serious woman with an infectious giggle entered my life. She has sparkly blue eyes that reflect her fun side. Her serious side, however, usually shows through first. As we ended our visits and opened our calendars to schedule another time together, she would say—*every time*—"I'll be there if the Lord wills." Frankly, that repeated comment drove me crazy. Why did she have to use that comment every time as a parting shot? Gradually I began to understand what she was saying: *God is in charge of my calendar.* In fact, she was quoting the New Testament book of James:

> Come now, you who say, "Today or tomorrow we will go into such and such a town and spend a year there and trade and make a profit"—yet you do not know what tomorrow will bring. What is your life? For you are a mist that appears for a little time and then vanishes. Instead you ought to say, "If the Lord wills, we will live and do this or that." As it is, you boast in your arrogance. All such boasting is evil (4:13-16).

So what's the best way to be effective in your use of time, energy, and resources? You may be surprised, but the answer isn't a clear-cut choice. Let me explain.

My personal history with churches is diverse. The walk from church to church and denomination to denomination has been incredibly enlarging for me. At each "stop," God taught me significant truths, and He showed me how to merge those truths. One church emphasized making a life plan, and I aligned myself with confident believers who made plans with God's guidance and stepped out boldly. In a later church experience, I was with a devoted group of Jesus followers who seldom made plans. They went from place to place and task to task as the Lord led them.

Which way was right? My conclusion was that both truths worked in God's management of my life. I plan to go to the stoplight and turn left, but I'm always ready and willing to get to that stoplight and hear Jesus say, "Go right." And that's what I do because He is in charge.

Me, Get Organized?

Emilie

Over the years I've received countless letters from women who want to know how to better manage their time. Either on their own or through coaxing from their husbands, children, or friends, they realize they will be more effective, more happy, more fulfilled if they could get their lives and priorities in order.

"Organized" means many things to many people. For some it's putting their papers in colored file folders. For others it's arranging spices, herbs, and seasonings in alphabetical order in a cupboard. For still others getting organized is the ability to quickly retrieve important papers that have been stored.

Even after writing 65 books with a combined total of more than 13,000 pages dealing with various topics of organization, I'm not sure I've covered all the bases for all women who want to be more efficient. As I share some timesaving ideas that will help you, I'm also hoping they'll spark ideas and plans of your own. This chapter is something of an "airplane flyover" of organizational ideas for busy wives and mothers. Are you ready to take off? Let's begin with you.

A Few Basic Requirements

Let's start with that harried-looking lady you've been seeing in your mirror lately. What is it about *you* that causes *you* to be disorganized? I find that organized women have a calmness and serenity about them that their disorganized sisters don't possess. Take an inventory in your life to see what may be causing confusion. Ask the Lord about it. He promised to give you insight and wisdom if you ask (James 1:5-8), and He will. And nobody in the universe knows you better.

See if you can't rid yourself of some of that internal clutter—or at least thin it down—before you move on. In some cases you might need to meet with your pastor or even a professional counselor. What you're looking for is someone who can help you unravel the root causes of your flustered mind and bewildered lifestyle.

Keep It Simple

There are many programs available out there—innumerable people with countless plans and formulas to share. My advice is to start with something simple. You don't want to spend all your time updating charts and graphs or administering complex plans.

Make Sure Everything Has a Designated Place

One of our family mottoes is, "Don't put it down, put it away." Here's another: "Don't pile it, file it." If there is no place for stuff to go, it's going to get piled. Piles can be very frustrating and discouraging when you're trying to get organized.

Store Like Items Together

Bob has his gardening supplies and tools together. I have my laundry in one place, my bill-paying tools in one area, my prayer basket and its tools in one basket, and my cups/saucers, drinking glasses, and dinnerware all in their general area. You don't want to spend precious time and energy bouncing from here to there getting ready for tasks.

Neat Doesn't Equal Organized

I recommend using notebook organizers. There are two things to remember: 1) write it down, and 2) read it. You're not accomplishing much if you write down that birthday date or that appointment on your calendar and then forget both because you didn't read your calendar. Remember to write *and* read. If your notebook easily lays flat, put it on a countertop or somewhere that will catch your eye several times a day.

Get Rid of Items You Don't Use

This is a tough one. Humanity seems to be roughly divided between "keepers" and "nonkeepers." Keepers are loathe to let anything go, reasoning they "might need it someday." (Some describe themselves as pack rats.) As time goes on, their cupboards fill up, their closets fill up, the bureau drawers fill up, their garages fill up, and before they know it, they're renting storage space because they don't have room for all their stuff!

Too many possessions weigh us down and fight against being organized. Jesus told us that "a man's life does not consist in the abundance of his possessions" (Luke 12:15 NIV). Just recently a man told me that after his wife passed away, he got rid of 95 percent of everything that had been stored in his basement—a huge pile of things. Now, five years later, he says he hasn't missed a single item.

You need to be a bit ruthless. Discard *all* unused possessions. When in doubt, throw it out. (Of course, that means recycling and donating to others and to charities as much as possible.) If something is just taking up space you still have to clean it and move it around—so get rid of it.

When the enthusiasm strikes to clean, start from the outside and work in. Take care of the clutter scattered around the room before digging into the closet. Starting with the closet first makes a double mess and may promote discouragement. To keep mess to a minimum when organizing, before you begin arrange three boxes nearby to categorize those things that shouldn't go back in. Label them "Give Away," "Put Away," and "Throw Away."

Work on one small section of a closet at a time. Don't empty an entire cluttered closet at once. The resulting chaos is sure to discourage you or put you off straightening things up entirely.

The most basic part of organization is knowing what to throw away. Invite an objective friend over to help you make those decisions (but don't argue!). The bottom line? Less is better than more. It saves you a lot of time and cleaning.

Invest in Organizational Tools

To be organized you need tools: bins, hooks, racks, containers, lazy Susans, and some of the myriad imaginative devices that have been dreamed up to help us conserve space. If you'll really make use of these items, most of them will be well worth your investment.

Involve the Entire Family

Home organization is not a one-woman job! Delegate tasks and responsibilities to other members of the family. My Bob takes care of all home and yard repairs. When something is broken, he is Mr. Fix-It. Depending on the ages of your children, you'll need to tailor-make their chores. Also change tasks frequently so kids don't get bored. Don't do something yourself that other members of the family can do. This will help you and be good for them by teaching them skills and letting them contribute to the household.

Keep Master Files

I use a three-ring binder, three-by-five file cards, and journals to keep track of all our possessions and tasks. You may think you'll never forget that you loaned that CD to Brad or the DVD to Christine, but trust me, you will. Write it down and keep the list in a place where you can't overlook it.

Continually Reevaluate Your System

Nothing is written in stone. See how other people do things, read a book to garner new ideas, evaluate your methods and organization aids, change those parts that aren't working. No plan is so good that it can't be tweaked and improved.

Liberally Employ Labels and Signs

If containers, bins, drawers, and shelves aren't labeled, family members won't be able to spot where things go. I also use color-coding to identify items belonging to various members of the family: blue for Bevan, red for Chad, and purple for Christine. Overkill, you say? You wouldn't believe how helpful and time-saving color-coding has been. Try it!

I use a fine-point paint pen to label clothing, glass and plastic jars, and wooden items. (Don't use water-based ink. It doesn't last.) You can also purchase a label maker. Writing your children's names on their school clothes and supplies also helps get those items returned when they're misplaced or lost.

From Donna

"Put it back where you got it from" was my daughter's first complete sentence. This simple habit keeps your space organized.

The key to organization is to work your way into these suggestions, implementing them one at a time. Don't try to do so much you get overwhelmed. Keep it simple, easy, and relaxed. Start where you are by implementing these basic suggestions. You can refine and expand as you go along.

Organization Begins Now

Yes, you must start organizing now. Don't let anybody tell you otherwise...being a homemaker, full-time or part-time, is a privilege and a gift. Please realize you have the greatest profession in the whole world. And how you organize your home and life will determine how effective and efficient you are in this honorable position.

Recently I saw this sign: *I had my home clean last week. I'm sorry you missed it!* Even though most of us would like a clean, orderly home because it brings pleasure and peace of mind, we need to remember that most homemakers don't have their homes in perfect order.

The modern woman, wife, and mom needs a lot of courage to

face the ordinary, daily tasks of managing a home. Let's make home-making an exciting adventure rather than drudgery. We can find satisfaction in jobs well done to the best of our abilities and energies. And even beyond satisfaction, we have our Lord's satisfaction to think of. Paul writes: "*Whatever you do,* whether in word or deed, do it all in the name of the Lord Jesus, giving thanks to God the Father through him" (Colossians 3:17 NIV).

Organization begins *now.* Do a little each day, and you'll be absolutely amazed at what happens in your home. Be consistent with your routine and organization. The following ideas will help. Read them more than once, and then add inspirations of your own. This "starter list" of quick ideas will keep you from backtracking and wasting valuable time. Think of time as money. You can save it or waste it, but you only get to spend it once.

A Few Timely Ideas

- Your inner drive toward order and clarity is much more powerful than the forces of chaos. Remember, the glass is half full, not half empty.

- It takes 21 consecutive days of doing a new task before it becomes a habit. Don't give up on day 15.

- Simplify and unclutter your life by saying no to good things and saving your yeses for the *best* things.

- Live a balanced life, saving some time for yourself. Stop all of that go-go-go. Be a person of "being" as well as a person of "doing."

- The specific elements of real order include a home in which it is easy to move around, with simple systems of handling paperwork and managing money.

- Any system of organization must be right for you. There is no "best way." What works so well for your best friend or sister may not work for you at all. Whatever methods you select must fit your style, your energy, and your schedule.

- Order and organization is not an "end" that you kill yourself to reach and maintain. It is a way to function effectively. Organization isn't a tape stretched across the finish line at a race. It's a better, more efficient way of running.

- In order to have order, you must think through and decide on your goals and purposes. Why do you do what you do?

- People don't plan to be failures, but they do plan if they're going to be successes.

- "Do the worst first" will help you get started. Once the worst is done, it's all downhill.

- Use the salami method to reach your goal. If the size of your project is overwhelming, tackle it a piece at a time. You wouldn't eat a salami whole, would you? You'd cut it into slices. Do the same thing with big projects.

- Share your goals with people who care about you and desire to help you. A goal is nothing more than a "dream with a deadline."

- Studies show that the success rate for people who write down their goals is about 90 times greater than for those who don't.

- Are you a morning person or a night person? Your efficiency may increase if you arrange your tasks as much as possible around the rhythms of your body. Try scheduling top-priority projects during your peak hours and routine work during your "low" times.

- Remember that notebook I spoke of earlier? Find one that works for you—either spiral bound or loose leaf, and small enough to carry around. This notebook will become your "master list"—a single, continuous list that replaces all those pieces of paper and sticky notes you might be used to. Use the notebook to keep track of errands, things to do or buy, and general notes about anything that requires action.

- Keep your list with you at all times. A list is worse than useless if you can't refer to it.

- On the other hand, beware of the tail-wagging-the-dog situation—when your appointment book, budget and expenditure records, filing system, and master list take more time to maintain than working out the problems they're supposed to solve.

- Keep a separate notebook to cope with complex, special situations—for example, enrolling a child in college, moving to a new home, organizing a family holiday.

- Don't be in a hurry to throw away notebook pages that have been completed. That stove part you ordered two months ago may be wrong when it arrives, and you may have to call the same people again.

- List 10 goals you want to attain by the end of the year—and then do them.

- Keep a daily "to do" list. Make up a new one each morning. Include tasks you specifically hope to accomplish—deadlines and appointments, as well as items from your master list. Give each task a priority number—1, 2, 3. Do them in order.

- Assign jobs and responsibilities within the family. Kids ages two to four can put dirty clothes in the hamper or match socks; ages four to seven can dress themselves and clear the table; those over eight can put away toys and do many chores reasonably well.

- Set up your own area for your lists, calendars, menus, and so forth. Announce to everyone this is *your* workplace.

- Start now—no matter what. If you have a call to make, start dialing. Have a letter to write? Sit down at the computer and start inputting.

- Buy a small basket or plastic bin for the various members of your family. I color-code these for my family members. Hang the baskets near the coat closet, using them as a repository for gloves, mittens, winter scarves, and other small items.

- Set up an emergency shelf out of reach of small children. Equip it with flashlights, candles (use votive candles in glass holders or battery-operated candles for safety), matches, a first-aid kit, and an index card with emergency telephone numbers. Make sure babysitters know where the shelf is.

- Make a list of three things you want to do. Next to each item, write two reasons why you're not doing it. Now change the two negatives into two positives. The ability to turn a negative attitude into a positive one is a key to self-organization.

- An easy way to organize your handbag is to have separate little purses—one for cosmetics, one for food items (mints, gum, etc.), and one for bits of papers and business cards. Another can be for Band-Aids, nail clippers, nail file, nail polish, and pills. All these little bags go into your big purse.

- Never have time to read all the magazine articles you would like? When you receive a magazine go through it quickly, tear out articles you find interesting, and file them away for future reading. And then recycle the rest of the magazine! There are few things that add to unsightly clutter like a stack of old magazines.

From Kay

Get the children involved in setting the table. Let them pick the tablecloth and napkins and theme. How about a picture for Daddy? If they like coloring, let them decorate white paper napkins. Make sure Daddy notices and comments.

- Here's a good tip: Pick-up items and dust in each room for five minutes. Time yourself with a kitchen timer, and when you're done, you're done.

- To organize various booklets and pamphlets that come with cooking and home-care appliances, punch holes into self-sealing plastic bags so that they will fit into a three-ring notebook. Use one bag for each appliance.

- Select one shelf in the den or playroom for storing borrowed library books. You'll know where they are when it's time to return them.

- Get rid of extra paper. Almost 90 percent of the paper in your home or office is never referred to again.

- The problem with storage closets and kitchen cabinets is remembering everything in them. Tape lists inside each door to save time and trouble.

- When you get a new reference book (such as a cookbook or gardening manual), attach a pocket inside the cover to store clippings, notes, or pictures about that subject.

- In that all-important master notebook of yours use an inexpensive monthly planner to keep track of gift giving. On each special date, note the name of the person, the occasion, and the gift given. Add sizes, color preferences, and any tips for future giving.

- Have a secret shelf for gifts. When you find something on sale or have time to shop, buy gifts in quantity, wrap them, and tag them for future giving.

Keys for Cleaning Closets

- No one has several free hours to clean out a closet. The key is to use 15-minute segments to accomplish a small task or make a dent in a larger one.

- As you weed out a closet, consider each item individually, asking, "Have I used this in the past year?" If the answer is yes, it's worth keeping another year. If no, discard it. "Does this item have sentimental or monetary value?" If yes, keep it.

- Will this come in handy *someday?* If you answer yes but have nothing specific in mind, don't keep it unless you have ample attic or basement storage space. A yes often means you're hanging on to clutter.

Finding Time

- Delegate some household work to other family members.

- Eliminate some of the work entirely. (You don't have to iron everything.)

- Make sure all your children contribute to running the household.

- Carefully plan the use of leisure time. Concentrate on doing those activities that give you real pleasure.

- Leave yourself open-ended time for spur-of-the-moment activities. Don't cram your day with appointments. Also leave "breathing room" between appointments.

- Do you have a lot of spare time or have trouble making good use of your spare time? Consider learning a new skill or cultivating a new friendship. Check your local newspaper to find groups you're interested in or volunteer somewhere.

- I practice a 45/15-minute rule that really helps. After every 45-minute work cycle, I take a 15-minute break or do something different, such as take a short walk, go outside for fresh air, call someone on the phone, get a drink of water. This keeps me renewed and fresh.

- Get the first appointment of the morning so you won't be delayed by someone ahead of you. You'll also still have most of the day left when you finish.

Before we leave the subject of time management, let's talk about "bits and pieces" of time. Many small chores can be accomplished in small increments of time. Some household chores can be done during "in-between times"—in between outings, appointments, or TV programs. For example, file your nails, make an appointment to see the dentist, or clean one shelf of that closet. You'll double your efforts if you do small tasks (such as writing a thank-you note) while engaged in another activity such as running a bath or waiting for a casserole to heat. Use a small tape recorder to give yourself reminders while putting on your makeup or taking the bus. Once you realize it takes only 15 minutes to change the sheets, you can fit this and similar tasks into available time slots.

While you're waiting in a doctor's office, you can pay bills. While riding the bus, write your shopping list or double-check this week's calendar. Here are some ideas for maximizing smaller chunks of time that fall into your lap.

What You Can Do in 5 Minutes

- Check your e-mail.
- Dash off a text message or a quick e-mail or two.
- Make an appointment.
- Water houseplants.
- Make out a party guest list.
- Order tickets for a concert or a ball game.
- Sew on a button.
- Sort mail.

What You Can Do in 10 Minutes

- Write an e-mail or letter.
- Pick out a birthday card.
- Repot a plant.
- Hand-wash some clothes.
- Straighten your desktop.
- Exercise.

What You Can Do in 30 Minutes

- Go through magazines and newspapers.
- Work on a craft project.
- Polish silver and brass.
- Vacuum three or four rooms.
- Weed a flower bed.

A Great Invention—The Telephone!

Why does a half-hour job often take twice as long as you thought it would? Probably because you estimated the actual working time but didn't take into account the preparation (getting out and putting away tools, for instance).

To save time and frustration, whenever possible use the telephone instead of making a trip. Phone to confirm appointments, to check if a store has the item you want, to learn business hours, and so on.

You might think e-mailing or writing a letter would be cheaper and more timesaving than picking up the phone and making a long-distance call. But that isn't necessarily true, especially when you consider how long it takes to write and how much your time is worth.

But what if you get stuck on the phone with someone who won't let go? Learn how to stop or cut off conversations without hurting people's feelings. For example, it's quite all right to say, "You know, this is not a good time for me. May I call you back?" (And then make sure you do.)

There is a paraphrase of a familiar scripture I particularly like. It's from the book of Ephesians:

> Live life, then, with a due sense of responsibility, not as men [and women] who do not know the meaning and purpose of life but as those who do. Make the best use of your time, despite all the difficulties of these days. Don't be vague but firmly grasp what you know to be the will of God (Ephesians 5:15-17 PHILLIPS).

When you put it in these terms, seeking to be better organized and more efficient in your use of time serves your family and pleases and blesses your Lord.

Moving Beyond the Organizing Tasks

Wonderful benefits flow from a more orderly, organized life that places first priority in knowing and walking with Christ. You'll experience a greater sense of peace. You'll find your life less fogged in by anxiety and nagging worries. You'll be blessed with more time to do what you *want* to do. All of these things are true. But getting organized isn't all about you.

From Donna

Listen to Emilie. Her home is a pure, restful delight and my favorite place away from my own home.

Once you get your head above the clouds of confusion and apprehension from an out-of-control schedule, once you bask in the sunlight and serenity of a more ordered life, you can reach out in love to others. The best, most joyous kind of giving comes from an overflowing heart.

Reaching Out with Love

Emilie

As daughters, wives, and mothers, all of us know what it means to give sacrificially, pouring out care and comfort into the lives of others when our own cup seems almost empty. But it's so different when we give out of abundance. When our own cup is full and spilling over, it's truly refreshing for others to be near us. That's the kind of life God envisions for every one of us. Paul writes, "May the God of hope fill you with all joy and peace as you trust in him, *so that you may overflow with hope* by the power of the Holy Spirit" (Romans 15:13 NIV). Jesus also spoke of a life of great abundance. Listen to His words in John 10:10 MSG: "A thief is only there to steal and kill and destroy. I came so they can have real and eternal life, more and better life than they ever dreamed of." And out of your abundance, you can uplift and bless others. Here's a wonderful suggestion.

The Love Basket

A "Love Basket" can be used for those very special times when you want to say "I love you" in a unique way. You can...

- fill it with food for dinner at the beach.
- take it to a ball game.

- bring it to an outdoor concert or the park with your family.
- make it a carrier of a surprise lunch or dinner in the backyard, your bedroom, or under a tree.
- take it in a car on a romantic getaway.
- place it on the doorstep of someone who needs encouragement and TLC.

Here is what you need to create a Love Basket.

- A basket. I've found that something heavy-duty works best—like a traditional picnic basket without a lid. Make sure it has a nice, sturdy handle.
- A tablecloth. It can be made from a piece of fabric you have around the house or even a sheet. I generally cut the tablecloth into a piece about 45-inches square. Line the inside of your basket with this cloth, letting it drape over the sides (so it looks really cute and special).
- Two fancy glasses with long stems. Trust me, these look *very* nice inside the basket.
- Four cloth napkins. I like to use ones with a small print, maybe gingham. Fluff up your napkins inside the top of the glasses, for a nice classy touch. At the event, one napkin will be used in the lap, and the other as a regular napkin.
- A candleholder and candle. Use something tall that shows over the top of the basket.
- Food:
  - nonalcoholic sparkling cider (which you can usually find in the juice department of a market)
  - loaf of French bread
  - cheese
  - salami
  - pickles

- mayonnaise or other sandwich spread
- other fancy, delectable items you or your guest might enjoy

• A spray of fresh, pretty flowers for a finishing touch to make your basket and "table" look "picture perfect" and inviting.

Now your basket is ready. But who will be on the receiving end of this extraordinary love gift? Let me offer you a few ideas.

Your Husband

One of the best and most welcome things you can do with your Love Basket is to bless your husband with it. Are you surprised? Well, when you think about it...who better to benefit from your lavish love and the abundance of your happy heart? And believe me, I practice what I preach! I've been putting together Love Baskets for my Bob for more than 50 years now.

Every wife can sense when her man is under stress, feeling a little blue, or just needs to be needed. Or perhaps your priorities have been out of order for awhile (something that happens to all of us), and you realize you haven't let him know how important he is to your life lately. These are times when a Love Basket is perfect.

From Kay

Because things change around the house and my husband doesn't always notice or comment, it was easy to think, "Why bother to do anything special?" But I've discovered love notes or surprise gifts, although not raved about, still speak volumes to Jack. How do I know? I hear it from others, it evokes an extra kiss, or his chest lifts. He knows he's special. Remember God's unsolicited gift of His Son said to us, "I love you."

I remember saying to my friend, "You know, my Bob needs a Love Basket tonight, and I'd like to put one together for him. Will you watch my kids for a few hours? The next time your husband needs a Love Basket, I'll watch your kids."

I still prepare Love Baskets for Bob. One time I called him at work in the morning and said, "Tonight I want to take you to a special restaurant you've never been to before. And it has your favorite food!"

"Well," he asked, "where is it?"

"I'm not going to tell you," I replied. "It's a special place in town. Can you be home by six o'clock?"

Do you know what? He got home by five-thirty!

Dinner on the Deck

We lived in a two-story house with a deck off our bedroom that overlooked the city, revealing a beautiful view of the city lights. We'd never had dinner up there before, so I took up a card table and a couple of folding chairs. I put the red-and-white gingham tablecloth on the table, as well as the candleholder and a red candle. Setting a beautiful I-love-you card on his plate, I went into the bedroom and lit a candle and had the music all ready to go.

It was the most beautiful restaurant in town that night.

Bob came through the front door with a smile. "Where are we going tonight?" he asked.

"It's a surprise."

"Do I have to change my clothes?"

"No, you're perfect just the way you are."

Stepping into the kitchen, I picked up the Love Basket filled with his favorite foods and covered with a cloth. I handed him the basket and said, "Follow me."

Having experienced previous Love Baskets, Bob knew that really special things were about to happen. He followed me upstairs with a spring in his step. Stepping out onto the deck, he heard the music and saw the candle burning on a beautifully set table. He opened the Love Basket with anticipation, taking out the fried chicken and an assortment of his favorite treats. As twilight fell and the city lights began to twinkle, we had a beautiful meal together just enjoying talking about this and that and looking and loving each other.

What was my Bob discovering? That I loved him, that he was important to me, and that I cared for him. I didn't share all the planning

I'd done or the effort I'd put into preparing our evening. He was aware that it took time and energy. I used this time to focus on him. And do you know what he felt like? Like a king. He knew he was a top priority in my life (after King Jesus, of course).

Love in Action

When she was courting Bill, my daughter Jenny made him a breakfast Love Basket. They had plans to drive to Los Angeles that day on business, so Jenny created a special breakfast that could be eaten in the car. She included flowers, orange juice, bran muffins, fresh strawberries, and sliced cantaloupe.

When Bill came to pick her up at six in the morning, he couldn't believe his eyes. He'd never seen anything like that before—especially so early in the day

Later Jenny told me, "Mom, it was so great. We got in the car and I did everything. I put the napkin in his lap, and we ate on the freeway. Bill loves the Love Basket.

From Donna

A simple snack and 30 minutes of "free time" after a long day at work said "love" to David.

This is a sure way to get a husband. At least it worked for Jenny! And it's blessed many, many others as well. Let me share with you two letters I've received from women who attended my time- and life-management seminars.

Dear Emilie,

I'm still thinking about the seminar and how much food for thought you offered. Everyone had to go away with treasures in thought, word, or deed. From your testimony to your organizing and all the helpful hints, I thank you. And the Love Basket—well, that was the best of them all.

Just ask my husband. He got his first one Saturday night. He absolutely loved it—sparkling apple cider, candlelight, and all. He was so thrilled that he says he'll have to thank you personally for that one. It was so much fun that we even had ours in the bedroom.

Love,

Peggy

Dear Emilie,

I've so much wanted to write and share with you. This has been on my heart for a long time. I've always been a very proud person. So in my relationship with my husband, I would never give my all. I guess I feared he would make fun of me or use me. I was very cold. I never said or did nice things for him.

In your seminar you shared with us about the Love Basket. It touched my heart. I talked with you after the seminar and shared with you that my husband had cancer. You said you would pray for us. Thank you for your prayers.

I decided to buy a basket and give my husband a Love Basket. I went all out. I decorated it and made a special meal. It was around Valentine's Day so I had a red tablecloth. I bought him a little present. I told him I had a surprise for him when he came home.

I really fixed myself up for him—set my hair and did my makeup. He liked that...I was usually a slob at home. He works nights, so when he walked in at 12:30 AM, he saw the table and the candlelight. I greeted him with a kiss. We had a wonderful time. He told me it was the nicest thing I'd ever done for him. I'll cherish that time forever.

My husband died a month later. I pray that if you share this letter with the ladies you speak to, it might touch someone's heart like mine had been touched. Set aside your pride and give to your loved ones.

A friend in Christ,

Denise

The poet Sholem Aleichem wrote:

> *Without love our life…*
> *a ship without a rudder…*
> *like a body without a soul.*

The apostle Paul put it even better:

> [Love] bears all things, believes all things, hopes all things, endures all things. Love never fails…Pursue love.[3]

That's a pretty wonderful life goal, isn't it? Pursue love and give as much as you possibly can. There are many ways to do that, and one of them comes in a basket!

Four

Building a Marriage
Without Regrets

Relating to Superman

Emilie

You would think that after 52 years of marriage, Bob and I would have it all together. Everything figured out. Everything wired. Everything humming along like a well-oiled machine. That's a nice thought, but marriage is not a machine. It's a human relationship, and every relationship needs work, care, and attention—and sometimes suffers from neglect and withers a bit through indifference.

To this day Bob and I put daily thought, effort, and prayer into our relationship. Are there still speed bumps along our marriage highway? Of course there are. And those are times when we need to humble ourselves before God and each other to make things right. And Bob and I not only live together as husband and wife, but we also work together. Many women told me it would be a disaster working with their husbands, that it would be way too stressful and frustrating. Yet Bob and I have worked together since 1982, and though we'll never be perfect, we've established a way of working in harmony and love toward goals we value and desire.

Bob's strengths compensate for my weaknesses, and my strengths compensate for his weaknesses. We balance one another and help each other in those areas where each of us needs the most help. Isn't that what Solomon was talking about in the book of Ecclesiastes?

"Two are better than one because they have a good return for their labor. For if either of them falls, the one will lift up his companion.

But woe to the one who falls when there is not another to lift him up" (4:9-10). Bob and I understand one another's temperaments, we know each other's quirks, and we're aware of each other's uniquenesses.

We also know each other's needs. And one of the most important words of counsel I want to give you in this brief chapter is simply this: *Let your man know you need him.*

"Well, Emilie," you say, "I think he already knows that."

Are you sure? It's like that old cliché about the man who never says "I love you" to his wife. "Why should I?" he grouses. "I told her I loved her on our wedding day 49 years ago, and if that ever changes, I'll let her know." That wouldn't cut it with you, would it? Why? Because you want to *hear* those crucial words. You want him to look you in the eyes and speak those words to you from his heart as often as possible. And when he does, it fulfills something deep inside you.

When my Bob tells me he loves me, it feels like everything is right in my world—no matter what else is going on. Admittedly I've had to work with him on this communication through the years. I've told him, "Honey, if you tell me you love me every day, I'll be a happy woman the rest of my life."

And it's really no different for a man. He also needs to hear you say "I love you." And he also needs to hear you admit you need him. Being needed is a vital part of a man's makeup.

The Big Red "S"

I vividly remember a day years ago when Bob came home from

work feeling really down. He was teaching school at the time, and something negative must have happened that day because it was unusual for him to walk through the front door with his eyes downcast. Frankly I'd had about all I could handle that day too. At that time we had five children, all under the age of five. (We were taking care of a relative's three children.) And unlike my husband's job, mine never stopped. I was never "off for the night." Mothers of young children are on duty 24/7.

In spite of all my responsibilities with the little ones, I always made sure I had a wonderful dinner on the table when Bob walked through the door. Slouching at the dining room table that night he said, "You know what? All I'm ever good for around here is a paycheck."

Of course that wasn't true at all. I wanted and needed him in a thousand ways. But in all my busyness and in all my devotion to my home and to the children, I evidently neglected to let him know that. And if Bob felt it inside enough to speak about it, I knew that was the way he really saw things right then.

I turned the situation around and around in my mind. A few days later I was shopping at a variety store and pushed my cart down the men's clothing aisle. I drove right by a display of men's colored T-shirts when something registered in my mind. I stopped and backed up.

On the top of the stack was a blue T-shirt with a big red "S" in a bright yellow shield on the chest. I smiled. I knew I'd found something that would tell my Bob he was needed for much, much more than "bringing home the bacon." I bought the shirt in his size, came home, took it upstairs, and laid it across his pillow on the bed. That evening I watched him out of the corner of my eye as he walked up the stairs to the bedroom. Quietly I went up behind him, peeking around the bedroom door to see his reaction.

First he paused. Then he laughed. And then he picked it up, walked over to the mirror on the closet door, held up the shirt in front of him, and began posing—lifting up his chin and sticking out his chest in a classic Superman pose.

I was telling him, "I need you, honey. You're a man—and a man's man. You're my Superman, and you do everything for me and our family."

A Matter of Trust

"Two are better than one." This is a nugget of Bible wisdom, and it applies to marriage. When you and your husband truly begin working together as a team, you can accomplish so much more than you could ever accomplish alone. Sometimes I need a masculine point of view, and sometimes Bob needs to see the feminine viewpoint. We balance each other. I'm a better woman because of him, and he's a better man because of me. I don't have his strengths, and he doesn't have my strengths. And we've learned to let each other achieve satisfaction and success in our areas of strength.

One of the things I do in our marriage is let Bob know I appreciate the way he protects our family. Through the years I've affirmed him in that role. But as with most valuable truths, I had to learn to do that. Early in our marriage we lived near a busy intersection with no stoplights. We had to negotiate it practically every day. Trying to turn onto that busy thoroughfare from our street made a nervous wreck out of me. The cars came so fast—from both directions—and we had to merge quickly with speeding traffic. To make the left turn we needed, we often had to wait a long time for appropriate gaps in the traffic.

As a rule I'm a more cautious driver than Bob. And in situations where I would typically wait for a better opening, he stomped on the accelerator and darted into the flow of traffic. Frankly, it scared me, and I used to grip the passenger side armrest and close my eyes tightly when he took off. We've never had any real problems or any accidents related to Bob's quick-reflex driving style, but it frightened me and I told him so.

Finally, after weeks of this, it dawned on me that I was basically telling him I didn't trust him. Being a man, that bothered Bob. So I swallowed hard and resolved to change my behavior at that intersection the next time we approached it. And that's just what I did.

Instead of tensing up and looking quickly back and forth or closing my eyes, I forced myself to relax and leave the driving (and my fate) in his hands.

After he slipped the car smoothly into what looked to me like an incredibly small gap in traffic, I said nothing, trying to be the very picture of relaxation and ease. I'll always remember that moment. Bob shot me a quick glance and said, "Well? You didn't say anything to me this time."

I replied, "You know, honey, I trust you."

"Hmmm" was all he said. But I could see my words had an effect. There have been other situations in driving when I saw things one way and he saw things in another, and because he was driving, we went with his instincts rather than mine. Yes, sometimes it's very difficult to sit there, trust him, and submit to his decision making. But that is exactly what God asks me to do as his wife.

If we can't yield to our husband's leadership in small situations, how obedient will we be to God in really big situations? This doesn't imply that as women and wives we're inferior to our husbands in any way. No, it simply means God established a certain hierarchy or chain of command in the family, and He promised to bless those who obey and follow His Word.

One day I was listening to Dr. Chuck Swindoll on the radio, and I really got a kick out of what he was sharing. He said there are three rings in every marriage: the engagement ring, the wedding ring, and the "suffer ring." We will all have some suffering in our lives and in our marriages, and many times we women are the ones who "suffer in silence" as we seek to honor our spouses and the Word of God. At the same time, if we were to ask a group of men about silent suffering, they would probably say they're the ones who usually take it on the chin.

R-E-S-P-E-C-T

Shortly after we began working together, Bob and I were doing a seminar at a church. He was going back and forth from the car, carrying in the book table and boxes of books and other materials. Out in the parking lot a woman who thought she was being clever said to him, "Oh, you must be *Mrs.* Emilie Barnes."

What did this remark do to his ego? He laughed it off at the time, but inside he struggled. And through the years he's occasionally had to wrestle with the fact that I'm usually the one who is more well-known and upfront in our public ministry. He remains behind the scenes doing the logistics and legwork.

Bob has dealt with it because he knows that, for now, those are the roles God has given us, and this is where we are in life. I'm so proud of him for the way he's balanced his masculine ego needs with his servant's heart and love for Jesus Christ. His attitude encourages me to redouble my efforts to let him know that I need him, that he means everything to me, and that I couldn't go on in ministry without him.

From Emilie

If you're single and have read this far, keep turning the pages! There are truths you're learning that will prepare you for the man God may bring into your life.

Your man wants to know you truly admire and respect him. He may not get much respect at work, he may not get respect from the guys on his softball team, he may not get respect from his dad or mom or brothers and sisters, but *you* can shower him with respect and admiration.

In fact, that is exactly what the Bible tells us. Speaking to husbands and wives, the apostle Paul says, "Nevertheless, each individual among you also is to love his own wife even as himself, and the wife must see to it that she respects her husband" (Ephesians 5:33). Isn't it interesting that in this verse men are commanded to love their wives with an unselfish love, but Paul doesn't turn right around and say (as you might anticipate), "And wives, make sure you love your husbands too." No, the apostle makes the point that the wife needs to, first of all, show her husband respect. The Greek word Paul uses here for respect actually means "to revere" or "to be in awe of."

Obviously this could be carried to a ridiculous extreme, but I think what Paul is saying is that the wife must see to it that she honors her husband in her mind and in her actions. She needs to make sure she's not disrespecting, ridiculing, undercutting, or ignoring him. Respecting your husband is one of those biblical commands that goes directly cross-grain to political correctness and popular culture. You don't have to watch very many movies or TV shows or commercials to see that men—particularly married men and fathers—are portrayed as bumbling, fumbling, selfish, and stupid. It's always hip and smart these days to mock men and masculinity. And the idea of a wife truly respecting—actually revering—her husband? Well, what a preposterous, stone-age idea that would be.

But true followers of Jesus Christ have always been at odds with prevailing attitudes. Our Lord calls us to be radiant lights in a dark, dreary place and salt in a bland, tasteless world. Being wives who respect their husbands in the name and power of Christ is a mighty witness for Him in these perilous times.

How can you let your husband know he's your Superman? Occasionally ask him to help you in ways that make him feel strong. Maybe you could remove that jar lid if you banged on it, ran it under hot water, and worked on it for a while. But hand it to your husband. There isn't a husband in the world who doesn't feel good about using his strength to open a jar for his wife. Ask him to help you bring in the groceries. You could do this job very well yourself, but once in a while say, "Honey, will you please help me get these groceries in?" That's one way of telling him that he's the strong one, and he's the guy you depend on.

Make your man Superman, and he will make you Superwoman!

Ten Things to Love

What do you love about your husband? If someone asked me that years ago, I would have answered, "Well, lots of things. A million things." But I'd never really sat down and captured specific things about him. So when a friend challenged me to write down 10 things

I love about my husband, I took the challenge. This is what I wrote and gave to my Bob.

> I love you because you are my friend.
>
> I love your talent for writing.
>
> I love your generosity.
>
> I love the way you try so hard to please me.
>
> I love the way you love sports.
>
> I love being together with you.
>
> I love making your breakfast.
>
> I love your creativity.
>
> I love that you love the Lord most of all
>
> and I love that you love me.

I propped my note by his shaving mirror to encourage him and give him a lift to start his day. Why not do the same for your hubby?

Now I know very well that you may be reading this and feeling a pang of sorrow in your heart. "I don't like my husband's temperament. I don't like the way he dresses or behaves. And I don't like the way he treats me sometimes. I couldn't come up with 10 things I love. I'm not sure I could even come up with one thing I could really compliment him on." You may have been deeply hurt somewhere along the line, and there are some things you simply can't admire him for because they are glaringly in opposition to Jesus Christ and the loving standards promoted in God's Word.

Perhaps you're saying, "I would love to have a marriage like Donna has with David, or Kay has with Jack, or Emilie has with Bob, but that reality simply isn't here." Maybe at this point in your life you don't have a man who seems to care about improving, changing, or cooperating. But you do have a covenant. For better or worse, you are linked to this man by promises made in the presence of God. Although you may think things are "worse" rather than "better" now, the story isn't over yet. You haven't read the end of the book.

God knows the end of the story—every story—and you are very, very precious to Him as a woman. And if you know Jesus as your Savior and Lord, you are precious to Him as a much-loved daughter. If you love Him, and if you have been called into His plan and purpose, He has promised that somehow, some way, somewhere, someday, things in your life will work together for your good (Romans 8:28).

The fact is, you simply don't know what God is intending to do. You can't imagine how He plans to work things out. You can't fathom how your situation could turn around for the better. No one knows about tomorrow because the future lies with God and no one else. And God has a pretty strong track record of changing people's hearts and lives. In fact that's His specialty and delight. But no matter what happens in your marriage, the most important reality is that you will one day stand before Jesus Christ, your heavenly Bridegroom, and you'll long with everything in you to hear, "Well done, My good and faithful servant." This is a gentle reminder that God values and rewards faithfulness…not perfection.

If you can't think of any reason to respect or admire your husband other than God's command to do so, I urge you to focus on being pleasing to the Lord. He certainly loves you, feels great tenderness toward you, and deeply values and appreciates you. And while you're spending quiet time with the Lord, ask Him to show you something or some way that will help you respect your man. You might pray,

> God, this is the marriage I'm in, and I know You hate divorce because it destroys homes and families and lives. Lord, it's hard for me right now, as You know very well, but I want this marriage to be the best it can be. Show me how to be Your hands, Your feet, Your lips, and Your heart in this relationship so I can minister to my husband.

Maybe you've heard about a woman who was given the assignment of coming up with 10 reasons why she loved her husband. She was also told to share them with him. Their marriage had been a difficult one, and now they were old. She was very bitter. When she sat down to write something, she couldn't think of a single thing. Finally, after much thought, she came up with one small, positive thing. She said to her husband, "You know, I've never told you this before, but I want to thank you and say how much I appreciate the way you've taken care of our income tax returns all these years."

When she said this, her husband was stunned. Then he began to cry. It had been a very, very long time since he'd received a compliment or any positive words from her. An old country song says "stand by your man." And while many today scoff at the song and sentiment, what's the alternative? To stand in opposition to your man? To step away from your man? To belittle and ridicule your man? That would hurt him, hurt your children, and hurt you. It would significantly reduce any chance you might have for marital happiness.

Since your husband *is* the man you're going to live with, do everything you can to create a home and build a marriage that shines like a bright light in a discouraged and cynical world.

Younique Helper

Kay

Have you ever watched an adventure show on rivers or gone on a hike to find the "headwaters"? Every river, no matter how wide and how mighty it becomes as it nears the sea, begins somewhere. By following the watercourse upstream, you can trace its flow back to where it bubbles out of the ground as an artesian spring. At the headwaters, probably somewhere in snowcapped mountains, the water is pure.

That, of course, is what we have in the Creation story in the first two chapters of the book of Genesis. In simple narrative, the Bible sets forth the creation of earth, sky, stars, seas, plants, animals...and man and woman. In this brief account we see our first father and mother just as the Creator intended them to be—unpolluted by sin, unstained by godless thinking, selfish motives, and sinful desires. Humanity at the headwaters...sweet and pure.

Where do we come into the story as women? It's a fascinating account. Read it with me:

> Then the LORD God said, "It is not good for the man to be alone; I will make him a helper suitable for him."...So the LORD God caused a deep sleep to fall upon the man, and he slept; then He took one of his ribs and closed up the flesh at that place. The LORD God fashioned into a woman the rib

which He had taken from the man, and brought her to the man. The man said,

"This is now bone of my bones,
And flesh of my flesh;
She shall be called Woman,
Because she was taken out of Man"
(Genesis 2:18,21-23).

At these headwaters, right from the beginning, man and woman are different. God forms man from the dust of the earth, and then creates woman from the rib of the man. God created the man first, the woman second. Woman was created for man, and brought by God to the man. Even so, Genesis 1 tells us that both man and woman were created in the image of God, with the intent that together we would rule His creation (verses 26-28).

Woman was created by God as a helper, suitable for man, corresponding to man. One scholarly Hebrew work describes the word *helper* this way: "A wife is not a man's shadow or subordinate, but his other self, his 'helper,' in a sense which no other creature on earth can be."[1]

I often illustrate *helper* by spreading the fingers on both my hands and inserting them between one another to make the two hands look like one. I explain that usually where a man is strong, the woman is weaker, and where the man is weak, the woman is stronger. As a result, they are more complete as two than they would be as one.

Many recent studies have confirmed what most of us already know very well: The genders are different from the time they leave the womb. In spite of what militant feminists have told us over the last 30 years, men and women are distinctly different—down to the very cells in our bodies. And when we're together, we're more "fit" than when we're apart.

People often joke about how a man is wired to do one thing at a time, whereas women can multitask. One writer put it like this: "A single-tasking man can do one thing well at a time—like drink a cup of coffee. In the same amount of time a woman can drink *her* coffee and…make breakfast, make the children's sandwiches, organize the window cleaner, phone the office, dress the children, write a shopping list, iron a shirt, and de-flea the cat. Whether or not this is an advantage is subject to debate."[2]

Yes, I will admit differences between the sexes can be very frustrating—on both sides of the ledger. In the delightful musical *My Fair Lady,* Professor Henry Higgins sings, "Why can't a woman think like a man?" Well, there is a simple reason for that. She's *not* a man. And there are times when it's definitely to the advantage of everyone that a woman thinks like a woman. Yet different and distinct as men and women may be from one another, we are on totally equal footing in God's mind and in God's plan.

Why We Need God's Precepts

> The LORD fashioned into a woman the rib which He had taken
> from the man, and brought her to the man (Genesis 1:21).

Since God gave woman to man, the man should be a faithful steward of such a valuable and precious gift. There was a time not so very long ago when this innate responsibility could be seen in men's care and protection of women and children. In earlier days some called it "chivalry." In more recent days it was known as "common courtesy." In reality it was simply a culture responding to foundational truths from the Bible.

Men were the defenders of women and children even at the cost of their lives. They were the ones who went to war to defend the homeland and make it a safe place for their loved ones. Men were taught to walk on the street side of the sidewalk to protect women from traffic. Men did special things for women—doors were opened, chairs were pulled out, ladies and older people were given seats on public transportation. A man would even rise to his feet when a woman entered the room, and often the tone and content of his conversation changed.

This masculine role waned as women became more independent,

insisting they could make it apart from men. Men were treated more as an accessory than an integral and vital part of their lives. Irina Dunn, paraphrasing a philosopher's anti-religion quote, said in 1970, "A woman needs a man like a fish needs a bicycle." Some of this backlash against the traditional roles is understandable when you take into account how many women weren't being honored, valued, and cared for by the men in their lives. Because men became careless with their stewardship of their daughters and wives, a segment of women reacted in anger. And instead of listening to God and holding to His precepts of life, many listened to the indignant voices of feminists who'd had enough mistreatment.

Then men reacted to the women's reaction. They too should have been exercising spiritual leadership and shaping their lives according to God's clear instructions. Instead, many simply resigned their roles as leaders and protectors. They faded into the woodwork and went their own ways to please themselves. It was easier than trying to fight for a place and a role that was increasingly being denied and even tromped on.

Do you see how life breaks down when we depart from the principles and precepts of God's Word? Do you see how confused and polluted the stream of humanity has become since it left the headwaters in Eden? Men get careless and heedless of their stewardship...women in turn feel used and devalued and strike out for more independence...men in turn feel unneeded and unappreciated and walk away, saying, "What's the use?"

How desperately we need God's instruction and counsel in our daily lives to break this destructive cycle. A willingness to study and apply the clear teachings of Scripture will show men how to be men and women how to be women. And here's what's so wonderful about our faithful God. He will not only show us *what* we are to do, He will give us the wisdom and the power to walk in that truth every day by relying on Him. As Paul reminds us, "It is God who is at work in you, both to will and to work for His good pleasure" (Philippians 2:13). Years ago J.B. Phillips paraphrased that verse to read: "It is God who is at work within you, giving you the will and the power to achieve his purpose" (PHILLIPS). We may be a long way from Eden, but people can be the men and women God called them to be.

How blessed we are when a husband understands his biblical role and steps up to the plate to be what God created him to be in his marriage and family. Adam said of Eve, "This is now bone of my bones, and flesh of my flesh." Woman was taken from man, and because of that, according to Ephesians 5:28-30, a husband is to love his wife as his own flesh—to nourish and cherish her. This is God's command to the husband in a marriage, and it's not an easy job. The fifth chapter of Ephesians is filled with imperatives for the husband. He is truly the more accountable in this passage, and it's because he's the man. His example is Jesus, and no bar is higher than that.

> *From Donna*
>
> A wife is not mute, but she is respectful and defers to her husband. It's simple...but not easy.

Maybe your husband knows these things and maybe he doesn't, but you can cause his burden to be a little lighter by making his God-given responsibilities as easy and enjoyable as possible by being as loveable as you can.

Where "The Helper" Can Help Most

You've heard about the male ego?

Well, you've probably heard right.

Men's egos are fragile. They don't like to fail or feel inadequate in any situation. That's how God wired them. As author John Eldridge wrote in his bestseller for men *Wild at Heart,* every man needs to feel that "he has what it takes."

Where does "the helper" come in? How can you bless your man in this crucial area of his soul? Make sure he knows you respect and admire him. That alone will go a long way in helping your marriage excel.

In God's commands to the wife found in Ephesians 5:22 and 33, the apostle Paul covers men's two innate fears: being ruled over by a woman and being inadequate: "Wives be subject to your own husbands, as to the Lord" and "The wife must see to it that she respects her husband." Surprisingly, God doesn't command the wife to love her husband (although the Bible instructs older women to teach younger women how to do that—Titus 2:3-5). Instead, God gives wives two essentials: obey and respect their husbands.

What does this mean in practice? Author Shaunti Feldhahn points out that "men would rather feel unloved than inadequate and disrespected."[3] There it is! So God counters this by telling us to respect our mates. Until I understood that passage, in my naivety I thought it was my job to help God conquer Jack's ego. It was like a cold splash of water in the face when God hit me with Ephesians 5. If God gave men a built-in ego, who was I to help destroy it? Instead, I needed to respect it.

Another writer says it like this: "Inside every man is a secret fear that he lacks competence and courage…that he's not as manly as he should be. A man knows he is supposed to take a bullet for his family. A man knows he is supposed to fix whatever gets broken. When he's feeling powerless, he shuts down and withdraws."[4]

All this is to say that husbands have a lot on their shoulders caring for their wives and families. Therefore, the more you encourage your husband and let him know you appreciate his efforts, the stronger he will become…and so will your marriage relationship. So try it tonight. When all is quiet let him know you love, appreciate, and admire him.

Although he may be far from perfect in your eyes, surely there is something—even one thing—positive you can single out and express to him. You don't need to use a lot of words, just a few good affirming ones. And don't spoil the effect by qualifying your words with ifs, buts, or howevers. Tell him what you admire, and eventually you'll see more and more of his courage and confidence rise to the surface. The fear in you will diminish as you let him know he is succeeding, and he becomes stronger and more intent in his relationship with you. And if you can, tell him you're thankful God brought the two of you together.

Remember, dear one, God uses marriage as His heavenly sandpaper to smooth us like fine-grained wood into people solid and durable but rich and soft to the touch.

Now if your husband happens to respond to what you say by telling you how bad he's felt or how you've demolished him in the past, don't get defensive. Simply listen, ask his forgiveness, and affirm him again. Businessman Chris Schroder writes, "A man is like a hermit crab. If we (men) trot out our emotions and get burned, we'll roll right back into that shell and may not come back out. We can't be bullied or cajoled into sharing our emotions. We have to be seduced over a period of time until we feel safe."[5]

From Emilie

There are women out there who would love to have your husband. So be the woman he admires. Walk him to his car each morning as he leaves for work—and not in a bacon-stained bathrobe and dirty slippers. Regardless of your man's age, he still looks. Men are visual.

God has specially designed us women, His own daughters, to offer help to our husbands in ways so profound and transforming that no other influence (besides God!) even comes close. At the same time, we have the capacity to destroy a man so completely he may bear the scars forever. The choice of which we do is ours. Make your choice wisely as a woman of God.

The Priority of Sex

Now, dear daughter, I need to touch on one other way you are your husband's helper and completer. What I am about to share has been affirmed in many, many conversations with men across the country...some with tears in their eyes.

Men need sex. Sex is on their brain. Men are turned on by sight.

And even if they're looking at another woman, they want their wives to satisfy their desires. How thankful we ought to be that our husbands want us! But what if she refuses? What does he do with his desire? Think about this. Don't simply write it off, saying, "Let him get his desires under control. It's no big deal. He'll get over it."

It *is* a big deal to men, and that's why God speaks so directly to this issue. And if you'll recognize it, obey God, and meet your husband's needs, you will enhance your marriage, build up your husband's confidence, and strengthen his loyalty to you.

Please take a moment to read the following passage. As you read, consider underlining every reference to the wife (woman), and circle every reference to the husband (man). It will help you really see what God says.

> [1] Now concerning the things about which you wrote, it is good for a man not to touch a woman.
>
> [2] But because of immoralities, each man is to have his own wife, and each woman is to have her own husband.
>
> [3] The husband must fulfill his duty to his wife, and likewise also the wife to her husband.
>
> [4] The wife does not have authority over her own body, but the husband does; and likewise also the husband does not have authority over his own body, but the wife does.
>
> [5] Stop depriving one another, except by agreement for a time, so that you may devote yourselves to prayer, and come together again so that Satan will not tempt you because of your lack of self-control (1 Corinthians 7:1-5).

What did you see? Remember this is *God's* Word—not my words or the words of any other human. God created men the way He did, and God understands how men are wired. He was the electrician! Don't short-circuit what He did—it could cause your husband to burn. So don't light a fire you can't put out in a timely fashion.

What did you see in verse 1? For a man to touch a woman, Paul is saying, is to light a fire. And that is not to be done outside marriage.

For this reason, a man who can't control his desire needs to get married. In other words, sex is for marriage only. It's an integral, very important part of marriage.

The only thing that can interrupt the sexual relationship in a marriage, according to verse 5, is prayer! How about that? You may prefer prayer to sex, but God tells you even then you and your husband aren't to go without sex too long because it makes *both* of you vulnerable.

Years ago I made a commitment to never refuse my husband. I admit there have been times when I've tried to find out how serious he was, but I've never said no. Will you make that commitment, dear one? And what do you do when you're "not in the mood"? You do it for the Lord. Sometimes the bed becomes your altar. I promise, if you'll obey God and not deprive your husband, you won't regret it. You won't lie there with a guilty conscience. Instead there will be a smile on your face. Obedience brings blessing.

In Proverbs 5 King Solomon warns his son about the wiles of an immoral woman. Solomon tells him to drink water out of his own cistern, to let his wife's breasts satisfy him at all times. That's well and good…unless his wife refuses. What does he do if the "cistern" is barred from him? Sex was created by God for "the having" of children, but it was also designed for "the having" of pleasure. That means your husband's pleasure and yours. Now as I say this, please know I'm not talking about perverted sexual pleasure. (If you need help and information on that subject, please read my book *The Truth About Sex*.)[6]

Before I leave this subject, I want to remind you of what I said a page or two back: *Men are turned on by sight.* How you look is important. I'm not saying this to make you obsess about every curve, wrinkle, pound, or gray hair. Just remember to consider the eyes of your husband in how you dress, what you wear to bed, and the lingerie you buy. (The color of your hair is pretty easy to change. Don't you wish other issues were that way?)

I encourage you to not let yourself go. Be kind to your husband. Dress for him. What lights his fire? What pleases him when you're in public? What makes him proud to introduce you as his wife? I'm in my 70s, and I keep myself looking as good as I can. Jack is in his 80s, and he looks great for his age. The other night he asked me if I'd gained a little weight. He's in his 80s, and he still notices a little extra flesh around my waist! I was tempted to point out his tummy—but I didn't! Really, I couldn't help but smile. The way I look is still important to him...and I do keep myself in pretty good shape. Jack wants me to stay lookin' good. No matter how old he may be, a man is a man, and his eyes will always be drawn to an attractive woman. Be that woman to him.

Five

Parenting with Purpose

The Art of Motherhood

Donna

A few years ago, by amazing happenstance, I found myself alone in Paris for a few days. It was summer, the air was soft and fragrant, and I walked, read, and ate outdoors. (An Otto motto: "Everything is better outdoors.") Every city has its unique atmosphere, and that is certainly true of Paris. As I strolled the city streets and neighborhoods, I allowed myself to absorb the sights, sounds, and smells of this very artsy place.

On one of those days I carefully planned a Sabbath rest in a well-chosen spot on the River Seine. Arranging my journal, sketch pad, Bible, pens, and paper around me, I settled myself and planned to spend hours in that peaceful place. Propped up by one of the walls of a footbridge on the strolling path at the edge of the river, and across from an ornate nineteenth century building, I prayed, wrote, thought, and sketched. I was very pleased at how the black ink picture of the buildings surrounded by trees turned out. After six delicious hours I got up to leave, taking my art, supplies, notes, and thoughts with me.

Are you impressed? Have you formed a mental picture of me as an artist? Are you wondering if any of my works have been published or are hanging in galleries? Perhaps you picture me sketching and painting my way through life—complete with a studio, oil paints, tins of brushes, palettes of color, and a paint-speckled smock. If that's what you thought, you're wrong—and you would also be right…in a sense.

Actually, I am an artist—and I want to help you see that you are too! No, you won't find Donna Otto prints available on the Internet or gracing the walls of museums. That would be nice, of course, but that would be insignificant compared to the reality of my life. I am first a wife and then a mother, and that makes me an artist of note. My studio is my home, and my canvases are the hearts and memories of those I love most. You can see my best work in Arizona, on the property my husband and I have lived on for the last 30 years.

From Kay

Your Father is the Creator—ask Him to show you how to decorate your home with what He provides. This gives home a special meaning and a sense of ownership and pride—the proper kind!

The rosebushes and fruit trees create a backdrop for our lives. You can see my artist's eye in the way I set my table and present my meals. You can note the colors and textures in the scarves, wedding blankets, baptismal blankets, dresses, golf covers, and mittens I knit and crochet. The order of my cabinets, closets, and bookshelves might remind you of a precise portrait that shows each strand of hair on the subject's head and each fold in her garment.

My "fans" have grown as I've aged, and the price for my work continues to soar. I am no Monet or John Singer Sargent. I'm a wife, a mother, and the maker of a home. The choice I made to make a home for a lifetime gives me a place to create works of art in varied mediums and environments. And please know this: My work will outlive Rembrandts and Picassos!

Art and Intentionality

"Well," you say, "that's fine for you, Donna. But I'm not creative like that."

Yes, you are!

The Creator God who made everything also created you. And He placed within you a divine spark of His creative power—whether or not you acknowledge it, and whether or not you choose to draw it out and develop it.

Kay taught us about the biblical priority of being "keepers at home" by drawing on the biblical books of Titus and 1 Timothy. She shared that God has called you to prepare a house like His house, a home like His home—a beautiful picture and foretaste of what is yet to come. By doing this you bring pleasure to God's heart and honor to His name. The biblical term used for "keep house" actually means "to govern or manage a house or the domestic affairs of a family."

You are the master of the house; your home is your domain. Within that domain, God calls you to exercise the creativity He's placed within you. You're to be an artist with the most important commission of all: bringing out the beauty of family and home.

The Art of Diagnosis

Walking the uncommon path and allowing your uniqueness to shine are so noticeable in the art of parenting. Just as an artist starts with a blank canvas, so a mother starts with her children. Actually, children aren't as "blank" as people once thought. They have their God-given DNA and individual bents and talents. A big part of the mothering task is to draw forth—to uncover—God's design. That's where the "art of diagnosis" comes into play. In a way, diagnosis is art. You have to pay attention to the details, figure out the foreground and background, and see how everything fits together.

Some years ago I woke up in the night in such pain that I cried out loud, scaring David and me. The pain was so intense I couldn't move on my own. David carefully scooped me up and carted me to the emergency room. Although the doctors on duty were kind and concerned, they couldn't figure out what was wrong. Over the next six weeks I was weighed, undressed, poked, and prodded by a dozen doctors in fields ranging from neurology to gynecology. No one could ascertain the problem. Wondering if I would ever find out what was causing this terrible pain, I finally scheduled an appointment with a physical therapist.

I hobbled into her office. She looked me over head to foot, commanded me to sit down, to cross my legs, to get up and walk across the room, and finally to lie down on the examining table. Everything I did caused me pain, and she could see that. Finally she sat me in a chair and reeled off her conclusions and suggestions for treatment. Within 90 minutes I finished my first treatment and experienced my first relief from that grinding pain. With each subsequent treatment I got better and better.

What had this professional done? She diagnosed my condition, and she treated it. She also showed me how to take care of myself.

I believe mothering is a similar process.

Leaning hard on the Lord for wisdom and insight into the life of your child, the artist in you begins to create tools for teaching, training, touching, making opportunities, education, and finding experiences that will foster and draw forth God's design for your child.

I love the story of the patriarch Jacob. On his deathbed he called each of his 12 sons to his side. "Gather yourselves together," he told them, "that I may tell you what shall happen to you in days to come" (Genesis 49:1). What followed was an amazing glimpse into the future of each of these men. It was both prophetic and incredibly insightful.

"Reuben, you are…"

"Simeon and Levi are…"

"Judah, your brothers will…"

"Zebulon shall…"

"Issachar is…"

"Dan shall…"

"Gad…shall…"

"Asher's food shall…"

"Naphtali is..."

"Joseph is..."

"Benjamin is..."

As God reveals the bent, the distinctives, and even the areas that need to be strengthened in the budding life of your son or daughter, you'll be able to draw those things out by your counsel, correction, and affirmations. If that isn't fine art, I don't know what is! Here are some ideas to get perspective on your subjects.

Ask the Creator every day to give you fresh ideas and wisdom about knowing and guiding your little ones.

Listen to your kids speak to one another and their friends in the car as you drive them to school or dance lessons or soccer practice. Be an active participant in conversations. Ask questions. Limit the use of technology (both yours and theirs) during times together. Hear the tone of their voices, and ask God to help you discern what's going on in their hearts.

Watch how they walk, talk, smile, and cry. Look for changes. Be aware of attitudes. Note unusual behaviors that may indicate distress or potential problems with drugs, alcohol, eating disorders, coping skills. Then sensitively open up a dialog on what you're seeing.

Provide and insist on a quiet-time hour. We are a nation of noise, and that trend is growing exponentially. How many walkers and joggers do you see with iPod earphones stuck in their ears? And have you noticed people in public talking and gesturing to empty air? When you get closer you see the telltale miniature phone clipped on their ears.

In an era when noise and talk and messaging are all around us, it's more important than ever to encourage your children to be alone with their thoughts, themselves, and their God. And "alone and quiet" doesn't mean having the iPod on its lowest setting.

The Art of Being a Family

In the New Testament book of Colossians, the apostle Paul spells out very clearly what being a family is all about:

> Wives, submit to your husbands, as is fitting in the Lord. Husbands, love your wives, and do not be harsh with them. Children, obey your parents in everything, for this pleases the Lord. Fathers, do not provoke your children, lest they become discouraged (3:18-21).

All the elements of a family stated in one paragraph! *Husband. Wife. Parents. Children.* And the apostle not only names each family role, he also tells us the task each has been designed to accomplish.

Husbands are to love.

Wives are to submit and respect.

Parents are not to provoke, incite, or abuse.

Children are to obey.

These conclusions didn't require a government commission, a blue-ribbon panel, a highly paid team of consultants, or a university study. The Bible makes it plain and simple for those who follow its instructions, counsel, and commands. And for those who love Scripture, you know this is only scratching the surface of the Bible's wisdom. From cover to cover it overflows with insights and truths for cultivating the art of family living. Here are more insights:

> We proved to be gentle among you, as a nursing mother tenderly cares for her own children...Just as you know we were exhorting and encouraging and imploring each one of you as a father would his own children, so that you would walk in a manner worthy of the God who calls you into His own kingdom and glory (1 Thessalonians 2:7,11-12 NASB).

In the space of five verses—and basically talking about something else—Paul paints a beautiful portrait of a mother and a father. A mother is gentle and cares for her children. The Greek word used for *cares* means to "warm them," like a mother hen warms her chicks under her wings. It implies cherishing and tenderness. A father helps his children by encouraging, comforting, and urging them to walk straighter, reach higher, and try harder.

The more time you spend in the pages of God's Word, the more you will see God's portrait of a family emerge with vibrant colors, wonderful details, and picture-perfect clarity.

The Art of Being a Servant

Children are a gift from God, and raising them is an act of service to Him. He's given you the authority—indeed, the responsibility—to teach and train them. You hold two positions: parent-in-charge and servant-leader. Use your God-given authority with great care. On the other hand, don't allow your determination to be a servant-leader make you a slave to your children's demands. When a child is consistently demanding and asserting his or her desires with bad behavior, the child wants to be in charge. And that is damaging to the entire family. God intended parents to be servants, not slaves.

The Art of the Table

Family mealtimes can be a special time and place for kindness and caring for each other. Make table conversation lively, memorable, and creative, but don't forget to promote thoughtfulness through man-ners. Teaching "please," "thank you," and "napkin in your lap" points your child to a positive, courteous way of life. Courtesy counts.

From Emilie

When Donna talks about how a mother hen warms her chicks under her wings, I so agree. Bob and I used to have a rooster and five hens. First the hen meets a rooster. Then she lays eggs and sets on them patiently. After they hatch, she doesn't let them stray. When it's time, she walks them around. One day she tells them they've learned all she can teach them. She cuts the apron strings and lets them live their lives, mistakes and all.

The Art of "Making Sunday Special"

In the 1980s Karen Mains authored a book called *Making Sunday Special*. Many twenty-first-century churches no longer meet only on Sundays, but the principle of a Sabbath day holds true all the same. The art of being a family and instilling habits that last a lifetime calls us to acknowledge one day a week set apart for God, for your family, and for His family. Accomplishing this taps into your God-given creativity. Every family will approach this a little differently, but the key is to find traditions and routines that work for *your* family.

The Art of Building Memories

Some of our best memories grow spontaneously through unexpected occurrences. But you and your family can build a treasure house of even more happy memories if you pursue that goal. In other words (and as you've heard numerous times in this book), be intentional about it.

The secret is creating a *context* for memorable times. And this grows out of family experiences. You can set the stage for memory-making moments by providing parameters for regular fun and growing family together time. For more than 25 years my little family went Christmas caroling. I facilitated this experience by first calling friends we wanted to carol and arranging the night and time. I put out songbooks for a group song selection time. I made sure dinner was on time the night of our caroling adventure. I also gathered scarves and mittens for everyone. Once we were out the door, I let the experience happen. Now our daughter is grown and has a family of her own. And guess what? Our caroling party has doubled from three to six! This beautiful caroling experience provides rich fodder for conversation, nostalgia, and laughter as we relive memories and make new ones.

Family vacations provide fertile soil for lasting memories. Camping trips are a great idea. I heard about a man in his fifties who retains indelible memories of a camping trip when he was no older than five or six. What made it stick was the hilarious time they had "fishing" for chipmunks. They tied a piece of bread on the end of a fishing line (no hook), cast it out five or ten yards, and then waited until a chipmunk grabbed the bread and took off with it. Then they reeled them in! The greedy little animals wouldn't let go. This was a crazy incident someone dreamed up, but the family has laughed and talked about it for years, even decades.

If you reflect on pleasant memories of your past, you almost always find a specific person took the lead in creating the settings. Mom, you can be that key person. Plan ahead, engage your husband's and children's imaginations, and start building lifelong memories. If you hear one of your children saying to a friend, "We always do it this way," you know you've accomplished your goal.

The Art of Training and Teaching

Training

The training of a child's will is vital. Children who never learn to do things they don't want to will be hampered by that lack of discipline throughout life. Solomon wrote: "Listen to counsel and accept discipline, that you may be wise the rest of your days" (Proverbs 19:20 NASB). What a principle! If children accept instruction and listen to advice, the benefits continue for a lifetime!

The goal is to *train* for behavior, helping your sons and daughters respond with specific actions in certain circumstances. Training is all about "doing" before the children fully understand *why* they are doing the response. Training involves producing observable behavior.

Training a child is the parents' task; choosing is the child's task. When both come into play, the results can be more productive than you can imagine. In fact, as the Bible tells us, "Sound advice is a beacon, good teaching is a light, moral discipline is a life path" (Proverbs 6:23 MSG).

Teaching

Your goal in teaching is bringing forth the qualities of integrity, purity, virtue, honesty, honor, and trustworthiness in your sons and daughters. Oftentimes—really, *most* of the time—what you want to teach your children goes directly against the current of contemporary culture. And it's always harder to row a boat upstream. One of my lifelong mottoes is: "Right is right no matter how few people are doing it, and wrong is wrong no matter how many people are doing it."

Teaching and learning is woven into the Bible from beginning to end. As I mentioned earlier, the apostle Peter describes our learning process as "ever increasing." The book of Acts tells us how a godly couple invited a fiery young evangelist named Apollos into their home. They sat down with him and "explained to him the way of God more accurately" (18:26). In Psalm 71 an old man looks back across the years of his life and declares, "O God, from my youth you have taught me, and I still proclaim your wondrous deeds" (verse 17).

Teaching builds on training by imparting knowledge connected to trained behavior. What do I mean? Teaching is to know; training is to do. Teaching gives knowledge; training gives skill. Teaching fills the mind; training shapes the habit. Teaching gives the child what he doesn't have; training enables him to make use of what he possesses. We teach the Word of God, but we train someone to speak of it effectively. We can teach biblical truths, but we must train others how to find truth for themselves.

I've found that women generally lean either one way or another, toward teaching or training. Knowing yourself will help you make sure you accomplish both. A teacher focuses on explaining why, and a trainer expects a rote or learned response. Which is your style? What are the pluses and minuses of your style? Is there a way to lessen any negatives?

A Final Thought

It may be a cliché, but that doesn't diminish the truth one little bit: *Children grow up fast.* Don't miss the privilege of practicing the art of motherhood. When you really stop to think about it, life speeds by at a blinding pace. God has given us one shot at living on this broken planet—just a few brief years, and then we're off into eternity. We have one brief opportunity to serve and love Him on earth while we serve and love our families...and then that opportunity is gone forever. I like this paraphrase of wisdom from the book of James: "You don't know the first thing about tomorrow. You're nothing but a wisp of fog, catching a brief bit of sun before disappearing" (4:14 MSG).

The "chief end of man"—our very reason for living—is to bring glory to God. That runs counter to the direction of secular society. It's as though the world is spinning in one direction and God is calling us to spin the opposite way. Today's culture makes light of women who choose to stay at home, manage their households, and devote their lives to their families. But this is a beautiful choice in the eyes of God. Receiving God's "Well done!" is worth more than any accolades or earthly rewards.

Children!

Kay

God knows I can't get pregnant in my seventies, but I'll be honest with you…I would love to raise a child again. (Although I'm not sure how thrilled Jack would be at this point!) I would love to enter that arena again and have women such as Emilie and Donna as mentors and teachers. There are so many things I would do now that I didn't do then to shape that child. I've learned so much through my experiences and my study of God's Word. It would be a thrill to invest again in the life of a little one, bringing him or her up in the "discipline and instruction of the Lord."

Donna has one child, though she wanted more. Emilie and Bob have two children. I have three. Each of our children and each of your children are unique creations of God, very different from one another. But every one of them is a gift of the Lord, a reward from the Almighty.

> Behold, children are a gift of the LORD, the fruit of the womb is a reward (Psalm 127:3).

That's good to remember in a day and a culture where children are sometimes regarded as a bother, an interruption, a burden to bear. Every day in our nation thousands of little ones are aborted, many times because women simply don't want the "inconvenience" of children in their lives. But children are not inconveniences! God's Word says they are gifts! They're a heritage from the Lord, a *reward* from a loving God.

One of the ladies at a recent conference found out she was pregnant at the age of 44. Was it a shock to her and her husband? You'd better believe it. Did it mean a change of plans in their life? Without doubt. But they view this occurrence as a gift from God. No person is an "accident," no matter what the circumstances of his or her birth or what that person has been told. Psalm 139 tells us this very clearly.

> You formed my inward parts;
> You wove me in my mother's womb.
> I will give thanks to You, for I am fearfully
>   and wonderfully made;
> Wonderful are Your works,
> And my soul knows it very well...
> And in Your book were all written
> The days that were ordained for me,
> When as yet there was not one of them
> (verses 13-14,16).

From the beginning of time and into the mysteries of eternity past, God knew which sperm and which egg would come together to form a particular child in your womb. He created your sons and your daughters to be exactly who they are. Before your children ever drew a first breath, God ordained all their days. And as your children grow, make sure they know and understand these truths. Your sons and daughters can walk through life with confidence knowing they are unique, eternal creations of a loving God and that they have distinct purposes in life.

As parents we're accountable to God for our stewardship over every gift He entrusts to us. And since children are precious gifts, we will one day have to explain our involvement in their lives to the Lord. God intended children to be nurtured in a family unit with a mother and a father. That's the pattern He devised. That's His plan. And when a husband and wife align themselves with God's original plan, they place themselves and their family in a position to receive great blessings. As Donna said, our families are beautiful works of art in the eyes of God and a testimony to His grace and strength.

No marriage and no family are perfect. People are sinful and imperfect. But when family life is done God's way, when God's presence and God's precepts are given ascendancy, your home can become a welcome haven. As I've mentioned, I believe we can experience a little bit of heaven on earth through our families and homes.

What a light a Christian marriage and a Christian family can be in a dark and broken world! The Bible says we live "in the midst of a crooked and perverse generation, among whom [we] appear as lights in the world, holding fast the word of life" (Philippians 2:15-16). We are children of the light, not children of the night. And we have within us the Light of life. What does that mean? As our world grows ever darker before the coming of our Lord Jesus, the Light from godly marriages and godly homes will shine brighter and brighter.

Have you ever sat by the window on an airliner on a night flight? When you're flying over wide stretches of farmland or prairie on a clear night you can look down into the darkness and see the twinkling light from a lone farmhouse. You may be thousands of feet above the land, but you can still see the light from one little home shining like a star. That's what a Christian home can be in any region, any city, any neighborhood.

In His Image

We spoke of children being gifts of God—gifts we are to steward and nurture in a prepared place. The children who come into our lives are created in our image as their parents. Your kids have your gene pool…and they may repeat the parts of your history that are negative unless you train and teach them differently. Going back to the "first family" in Genesis 5:3, it says of Adam that he "became the father of a son in his own likeness, according to his image, and named him Seth."

Over in the New Testament we read that "through one man [Adam] sin entered into the world, and death through sin, and so death spread to all men" (Romans 5:12). David said, "In sin my mother conceived me" (Psalm 51:5). In other words, he was born sinful in the image of his parents.

From Donna

Kay is so right. Each of us is born in the sinful image of our parents. It's hard to look at the brand-new "pink" or "blue" baby you've waited nine months for and call him or her a "sinner." Dear daughters of my heart, acknowledge your child's true nature early so you can pray for him or her and teach your little one God's ways.

So when you hold that beautiful little baby, you're cradling a precious little sinner. As that child grows up, you don't have to teach him or her how to lie, how to cheat, how to be selfish, or how to disobey. That's part of his or her inherent nature. What you do have to teach is how to tell the truth, how to be honest, how to give and share, and how to be obedient.

God wants children brought up in *His* image and likeness. And for a season of time, He's subcontracted the job to moms and dads. So how do you as a mom do that? How do you raise children in your image so they're formed into God's image? By training, teaching, and disciplining the children entrusted to your care. (Does this mean our kids will always turn out "godly"? Unfortunately no. Samuel's sons didn't turn out well, and neither did King David's. Each child chooses his or her path; however, it is your responsibility to do your part by praying and resting in God while you parent. And you can do that if you follow His precepts and remember God is far greater than your mistakes.)

Proverbs 22:6 tells us to "train up a child in the way he should go" and "even when he is old he will not depart from it." As you probably realize, this is not an ironclad promise in Scripture. It's a principle; it's wisdom; it's the way things usually work. I train my child because God trains me as His child. I instruct and teach my child because God's Holy Spirit instructs and teaches me through God's Word. I discipline my child because God disciplines me in love to save me from myself and turn me in the right direction. God is my pattern. I parent my children as my heavenly Father parents me.

When Solomon wrote "train up a child in the way he should go," the Hebrew word translated "train up" is *chanak*. It means "to inaugurate or initiate a child into the way he should go." The Amplified Bible translates this phrase, "Train up a child in the way he should go [and in keeping with his individual gift or bent], and when he is old he will not depart from it" (brackets in original).

The Hebrew word *chanak* used here for *train* means to dedicate. Only in Proverbs 22:6 is the verb translated "train." This seems to include the idea of setting aside, narrowing, or hedging in. Child-training involves "narrowing" a child's conduct away from evil and toward godliness.

Gleason L. Archer points out that *chanak* is similar to an Egyptian term, which means "to give to the gods" or "to set up something for divine service." Isn't that wonderful? You and I have the privilege of setting up our children for the service of the Lord. (Doesn't this remind you of Hannah with her little boy Samuel? See 1 Samuel 1.) Dr. Archer suggests that this gives *train* the following range of possible meanings: "To dedicate the child to God," "to prepare the child for his future responsibilities," "to exercise or train the child for adulthood."[1]

In respect to the phrase "in the way he should go," there are several possible interpretations. The generally accepted one is "the proper way," the path of wise, godly living that is emphasized frequently in Proverbs—basically, the way of wisdom. Bear in mind that this proverb is not a *carte blanche* guarantee from the Lord that your children will turn out right with God. As I said earlier, your children possess free will and must make their own decisions about whether to follow God and His Word. And remember, if they make professions of Christ but their lives don't demonstrate they are new creations in Christ (2 Corinthians 5:17), if there are no deeds to back up their statements, then their words were just professions and not a true saving relationship (Titus 1:16; 2:11-14; James 2:17; 1 John 3:10). Read 1 John and highlight the word "know," and you will see this for yourself.

I became a Christian before David, my third son, was born. I remember going before the Lord saying, "God, please help me understand this new son You've given me. Show me what David is all about. Show me his qualities. How should I discipline him? How should I teach him to know You?"

In answer to that prayer, I believe the Lord showed me David's potential as a leader. With that in mind, I chose stories of great leaders, both Christian and non-Christian, to read to him before bedtime. We learned about Abraham Lincoln, Gandhi, and others who were teachers and influencers and had impacts on their times. We found a series of books based on the life of Ivan, a brave young man who lived in Russia under the communist regime.

Some nights we'd both be tired, and I would say, "Now honey, I'm only going to do one chapter tonight." But then the story would get so exciting I'd say, "Well, maybe just one more chapter." We'd end up reading three or four! This was our special time together each day. I was training my child according to his bent, which God revealed to me.

Understanding your child's personality, temperament, and particular needs is very important. Ask God, "Who is this child? What is this child's bent? What do You have in mind for her? How do you want to use him?"

And all of this includes discipline, of course. In Ephesians 6:4 Paul tells us, "Fathers, do not provoke your children to anger, but bring them up in the discipline and instruction of the Lord." This applies to mothers too. Don't pressure your sons and daughters too much. Don't put them under such strain that they become frustrated and angry and allow resentment and bitterness to build up in their hearts. Instead Paul says, "Bring them up in the discipline and instruction of the Lord."

The Greek word for *discipline* is *paideia*. It's the sum of a child's training. You're not to just compel your child to toe the line physically, but you're also to teach. This is discipline that regulates; discipline that instructs, corrects, and shows the way. The word for *instruction* in Ephesians 6:4 is *nouthesia,* which means "to place in the mind." This could be interpreted as "correction by word of mouth." Paul reminded Timothy that "from childhood you have known the Holy Scriptures, which are able to make you wise for salvation through faith which is in Christ Jesus" (2 Timothy 3:15 NKJV).

So bring your children up in the discipline and nurture of the Lord. How do you do that? Maybe the best way is by heeding the words of Moses in Deuteronomy 6:6-9:

> These words, which I am commanding you today, shall be on your heart. You shall teach them diligently to your sons and shall talk of them when you sit in your house and when you walk by the way and when you lie down and when you rise up. You shall bind them as a sign on your hand and they shall be as frontals on your forehead. You shall write them on the doorposts of your house and on your gates.

Dear friend, *whatever you're doing, wherever you're going, make the Word of God and the knowledge of God part of your everyday life and conversation.* Weave the eternal truths of Scripture and the accounts of who God is and what He's done in your life through the fabric of everyday living. When you're at the breakfast table...when you're driving the kids to school or on the way home from soccer practice...when you're on a family hike, talk about the Lord! Talk about His Word. Talk about your experiences with Him and what He's shown you and taught you. And don't use a forced, formal, "Sunday voice." Make sharing about the Lord a natural part of life.

And when you're on your knees before the Lord in your quiet times of prayer and reflection, talk to Him about your little boy or little girl. Talk to Him about your teenager. Seek His insights and His counsel. Pursue His wisdom when you don't know what to do or which way to turn. Do you remember what it says in the book of James to those in the middle of trials? "If any of you lacks wisdom, let him ask of

God, who gives to all generously and without reproach, and it will be given to him" (1:6).

God has a greater interest in seeing your children shaped into His image than you do. If you ask Him for wisdom and insight in how to raise and instruct your children, He will give it to you. He will help you determine the course your sons and daughters should take…and give you ideas on how to start working toward that.

Mind and Conscience

One of the most important things you can do as a parent is to protect the minds of your children. Scripture says, "For as [a man] thinks in his heart, so is he" (Proverbs 23:7 NKJV). Be a guardian of those tender minds. Know what your children are being taught at school. But even more important than that, keep teaching them truth. Satan is a liar and the father of lies (John 8:44). His first recorded words in the Bible—to Eve in the Garden—were an outright lie, revealing his character and his intentions (Genesis 3:1).

Second, you want to help your children have pure consciences. The conscience is that which helps people know right from wrong, good from evil. If something is wrong, it should trouble us when we're about to misbehave, go against the knowledge of God, or resist His precepts for life. When we've sinned, the Holy Spirit will use our consciences to bring us to the point of conviction over that wrong.

Dear one, teach your children to have a fear of God—a strong respect for who He is and an absolute assurance that He means what He says. Job 28:28 says, "Behold, the fear of the Lord, that is wisdom; and to depart from evil is understanding." Read the Word of God with your children, discuss its precepts, and most of all, let them see you living and walking in the wholesome life-giving fear of the Lord. First Timothy 1:5 has a good word for us as parents: "The goal of our instruction is love from a pure heart and a good conscience and a sincere faith."

One of the best ways to instill the Word of God into the minds and hearts of your children so they have a "sincere faith" that will hold them for the rest of their lives is to teach them how to study inductively—to go straight to the Word of God to "discover truth for themselves." Children are perfectly capable of doing this if you teach them the skills of observing the text. The best way to do this is through the *Discover 4 Yourself* series of inductive studies written for children who can read. The transformations that take place through these studies truly demonstrate that God's Word is alive and powerful. Children are delighted they can study the Bible book by book and understand and remember it while having fun doing puzzles, projects, and plays. Adults so often underestimate children's great capacity to learn and their love of knowledge. When you teach your children to study inductively, you're giving them God's "plumb line" by which they can measure all they are taught. You're helping them have a biblical worldview and equipping them to stand against the pressures of culture and worldly wisdom.

Science has made such strides in studying the brain, and now that brain imaging is possible, we can understand why God, throughout His Word, talks of the importance of our minds. There is no doubt: *What we think influences our behavior.* Dr. Timothy R. Jennings describes an elaborate study evaluating violence levels in society before and after the introduction of television. Here are a few significant lines from his conclusion:

> After the introduction of TV, homicide rates in the U.S. increased by 93 percent from 1945 to 1974. During the same period, the homicide rate in Canada increased 92 percent. But in South Africa, in which TV did not appear until the 1970s, the homicide rates decreased by 7 percent from 1945 to 1974. Astoundingly, after the introduction of television in 1975 the homicide rate increased 130 percent.

> In April 2004 the professional journal *Pediatrics* published astounding research that revealed television watching by children increases their risk of developing attention deficit disorder. The amount of time a child watches television changes the brain.

The American Academy of Pediatrics recommends no television of any kind for a child under 2 years of age and strict limitation on older children.[2]

Other Critical Areas for Healthy Families

In our Youniquely Woman Finishing Schools, we go into some depth on the issues of sleep and nutrition in the lives of children. This is so worth your while to investigate because these two basic necessities radically affect a person's ability to think and react in ways that are emotionally responsible.

As women moved into the workforce it soon became apparent that the family was suffering nutritionally—and emotionally. It changed family routines by depriving people of needed sleep, the good nutrition of home-cooked meals, and the irreplaceable dynamics of a happy, relaxed family sitting around the table together at mealtimes.

The Priority of Nutrition

Food can heal, and food can kill. Generally speaking, today many of us are killing ourselves eating what we do. The increase in diseases among the young as well as the middle-aged verify this. According to Proverbs 31:14-15, it's the woman's responsibility to see that her family eats properly:

> She is like merchant ships;
> She brings her food from afar.
> She rises also while it is still night
> And gives food to her household
> And portions to her maidens.

"She brings her food from afar." That doesn't sound like fast food to me. This doesn't sound like grease-fried fast-food chicken, a sack of hamburgers, sugar-loaded beverages, a frozen pizza, or Pop-Tarts. Yes, it's difficult to do good nutrition on the run. It takes time to think through menus with an eye toward a good balance of nutrition. Time to stock the cupboards and refrigerator with wholesome foods. Time to get healthy fruits and vegetables ready to eat.

When you think of the limitless tons of fast, fatty, sugary, nutrition-empty foods that people consume every day, is it any wonder people are as fat as they are, as sick as they get, as mentally slow as they're becoming? SAT test scores among all students in the United States dropped 73 points! And it's no coincidence that a rash of diseases affecting the mind and nervous system have become epidemic. Think of the increase in fibromyalgia, Parkinson's, multiple sclerosis, and Alzheimer's.

In this limited space I can do little more than introduce you to this vital subject...and pray you will read and learn more. Carefully consider what you're eating and what you're feeding your family. If your children aren't getting well-balanced, home-cooked meals, and it's directly impacting their ability to think and reason and deal with life, what needs to be your priority, Mom?

These are your children. You're responsible for their health and welfare. Taking care of your children in all aspects isn't a grim duty or unhappy responsibility. As Donna and Emilie emphasized, family is precious and kids are a blessing. So make mealtimes the highlight of your family's day. Sit down at an attractive table and eat wholesome foods as you talk, talk, talk over the events of the day. (Please avoid controversial subjects. Conflict makes food stick in the throat.) The dinner table is the ideal place to discover more about each other by listening to your children reflect on the events of their lives and share what they look forward to and what they're worried about.

Even clean-up afterward can be a bonding experience. I had three sons—no female in the kitchen except me and the dog. My boys learned to set a table and wash the mixing bowls and pots and pans before we sat down to eat so cleaning the kitchen wasn't an overwhelming task after dinner. And what I did with my boys continues to pay off. When we have a family meal with 14 people around the table, the boys help clear the table and clean the kitchen. And their children do the same.

The Necessity of Sleep

You are what you eat, and you're also what you sleep. We're a sleep-deprived society, and it shows. Have you noticed how quickly people get angry, fly off the handle, and let you have it verbally or with gestures?

Sleep deprivation is a major issue for adults and children. It causes irritability, depression, memory loss, lethargy, low sex drive, poor grades, poor job performance, loss of employment, and marital problems. It bangs doors, pushes horns, stomps feet, screams, closes its eyes and nods before searching for more caffeine or sugar. It plays a role in traffic accidents, on-the-job accidents, and in more mishaps and disasters than we can imagine.

Kids are so scheduled, so programmed, so rushed, so up-and-out-the-door so early today that they look at showering as a time to relax. They're deprived of the sleep their growing bodies need and the rejuvenation that only sleep can bring. Preschoolers and school-aged children need 10 to 12 hours of sleep *every* night. Teens need 9 to 12 hours. A study at Northwestern University Medical Center of 510 children between the ages of 2 and 5 found that less sleep at night resulted in more behavioral problems during the day. Researchers have found that watching television is a major cause of sleep disturbance, leading to bedtime resistance, sleep onset delay, shorter sleep time, and anxiety about sleep. They also found that sleep problems escalate when children have televisions in their rooms.

Lawrence Epstein, MD, author of *The Harvard Medical School Guide to a Good Night's Sleep* says, "The link between sleep and health, and bad sleep and disease, is becoming clearer and clearer."[3] Unfortunately the sleep that is missed one night can't be made up the next night. Contrary to popular thought, it doesn't work that way. Once it's lost, it's gone forever. Sleep is when the body does its repair work—regenerates skin, blood and brain cells, and muscles. Sleep rehabilitates and heals. It takes sleep to release growth hormones in children and young adults, and it is sleep that rests the parts of the brain that control emotions and social reactions. Are you getting the picture?

I used to think it "wasn't spiritual" to sleep more than six hours, although I truly needed between eight and nine hours. So I pushed my tired body…and served the Lord. Then God spoke to my heart about what I call "presumptuous sin." The conversation went something like this: "If I made the body to require an average of eight hours of sleep, and you don't honor that…and even think that because you're serving Me you can abuse the body I made and not reap the consequences, isn't that presumptuous on your part?" You know the answer, don't you? I did too. Staying up late and getting up early is useless. "He gives to His beloved even in sleep" (Psalm 127:2).

The Priority of Laughter

Bible precepts for the family are vital, and we will indeed have to give an account of our stewardship over our children, those precious gifts from heaven, to the Lord. But that doesn't mean life has to be grim. I believe the atmosphere of a home means everything—and I'm not talking about air conditioning or allergens. Have you ever walked into a home and from the minute you stepped through the front door you felt the air was heavy? Could you feel the anger, the grief, the hurt, the bitterness, the tension? And so do the little ones who live under that roof. Conversely, have you been in a home where you sensed an immediate lightness? You could feel it in the smiles, the lighthearted banter, the looks of love, the affirming words, and the laughter that seems to have soaked into the very walls. It's a happy place to be. As Emilie says, it's a *welcoming* home.

In the book of Proverbs Solomon affirms that a happy, friendly, lighthearted home is good for emotional and physical health.

> Anxiety in a man's heart weighs it down,
> but a good word makes it glad.
>
> A happy heart makes the face cheerful,
> but heartache crushes the spirit.
>
> A cheerful look brings joy to the heart,
> and good news gives health to the bones.
>
> A joyful heart is good medicine,
> but a broken spirit dries up the bones.[4]

An upbeat atmosphere at home starts with a cheerful attitude in the morning. When my boys were little, I would go into their rooms singing happy nonsense: "When the red, red robin comes bob, bob, bobbin' along…Wake up, wake up, you sleepyhead. Get up! Get up! Get out of bed!…Look up and live. Live, love life, and be happy."

From Emilie

Bob and I are reaping what we sowed. Our kids, Jenny and Brad, are living with their families and following the wonderful traditions we established when they were young. It's delightful to see activities and values passed on to new generations.

Another way to brighten the home is to celebrate as much as possible. Special occasions call for special resourcefulness! Recently I was looking at some pictures and laughing at some of the cakes I made for special occasions. I would take a simple flat cake and let my creativity run wild. I decorated according to what the special person was in to. I dyed the frosting to go with the theme of the cake: green for grass, blue for water, and so on. I also added chopped nuts for paths. I'm sure you get the idea. One cake even had a road made of ground up chocolate and was complete with trucks and earth moving equipment. Another had an American flag, along with tanks and toy soldiers. I've had cakes with mermaids, cakes with sparklers, cakes with flowers, and at least one little princess cake for my granddaughter. I threw a party for her and invited all her friends. We wore pretty hats and did girl things. She was the princess!

Photographs bring back so many precious memories. My favorite ones are of our annual Christmas plays. All the grandchildren came over for a special overnight party sometime during the week before Christmas. We'd plan and rehearse a Christmas play. Every year it was a different story, but it always included the gospel message. Sometimes my robes and dressing gowns were worn by Mary and Joseph and the shepherds. One year my lace tablecloth served as Jesus' robe as He returned in glorious triumph to reign as King of kings.

As they continue to grow, my children and grandchildren remember many special things about our home. And the memories bring smiles to their faces and joy to their hearts. I hope my family members and friends say to each other, "We sure had fun, didn't we! And we still do!" As far as I'm concerned, that's a taste of heaven.

Everything I've presented in this chapter is to encourage you to make your family and home a priority. Honor God in everything you do and teach your kids about Him. I want you to look forward to the day Jesus comes or you go to meet Him and receive your reward according to your deeds (Revelation 22:12). May you receive a full measure for raising your kids for Him!

A Nitty-gritty Exercise

As we saw earlier, Proverbs 22:6 says,

> Train up a child in the way he should go,
> even when he is old he will not depart from it.

How Would You Have Your Child "Go"?

If you have questions about the qualities you want to see in your children, read through the book of Proverbs. (There's a chapter for every day of the month!) Notice the fruit of the Spirit in Galatians 5:22, look at the characteristics of love in 1 Corinthians 13, read Ephesians chapters 4 through 6, and peruse Colossians 3. Note what qualities are commended and condemned. Then, as you read through the Bible during your quiet times or study times, add to your list other qualities you want to see developed in your child. To help you, here's a little worksheet section.

Values I Want My Kids to Have

Character Qualities I Want to Promote in My Kids

How I Want My Kids to Behave

At home...

As guests...

In church...

In public...

With the elderly and people with special needs...

How I Want My Children to Treat My Husband and Me

Now...

When they're teens...

When they're adults...

When my husband and I are elderly...

Skills I Want My Kids to Develop

How I Want My Kids to Talk

To their peers…

To younger children…

To adults…

To those in authority…

The Relationship I Want My Children to Have with God

The Future for Younique Women

Strength and dignity are her clothing, and she smiles at the future. She opens her mouth in wisdom, and the teaching of kindness is on her tongue. She looks well to the ways of her household, and does not eat the bread of idleness. Her children rise up and bless her; her husband also, and he praises her, saying: "Many daughters have done nobly, but you excel them all." Charm is deceitful and beauty is vain, but a woman who fears the LORD, she shall be praised. Give her the product of her hands, and let her works praise her in the gates (Proverbs 31:25-31).

A woman who can smile at the future is a woman who lives and orders her todays in the light of tomorrow. Therefore, assess what it will take to achieve what you desire for your Lord, your marriage, your children, your extended family, yourself, and your community. Jot down your standards and priorities. I'd love to help you with this more, but space limits what we can do together. I encourage you to talk with your heavenly Father and your husband. As you seek God individually and jointly, He will lead you through His Holy Spirit.

Six

Nurturing Your
Spiritual Life

Making Time for Prayer

Donna

I'm grateful you've decided to read this chapter rather than hurriedly skipping over it when you saw the title. Making time for prayer can be a tough topic. And believe me, I understand. The idea of "making time" for *anything* sometimes seems overwhelming. Your days are already filled to the brim, and the idea of escaping to some mythical prayer closet for extended times of prayer seems idealistic at best and wildly improbable at worst.

We aren't cloistered nuns whose primary duties are to chant Scripture, meditate by the hour, and pray. How would we fit all that in—even if we knew how to do it? We're housekeepers, cooks, transportation directors, seamstresses, Sunday school teachers, den mothers, gardeners, storytellers, PTA volunteers, and full-time or part-time employees. *Whew!*

Caught up in each day's rat race the way we are, the only prayer life we seem to have time for is an occasional five-second prayer of desperation: "Oh Lord, please don't let *tonight* be the night Tom is bringing his boss home for dinner!" Or maybe, "Please, Lord, *please* let the baby sleep one hour this afternoon so I can clean the floors."

Fortunately our God is generous, loving, and—most of all—full of grace. He knows our hearts, and He knows the world in which we live. He doesn't have angels checking prayer meters in heaven. He doesn't require us to punch a time clock every time we talk to Him. If we stay as close to Him as possible while we work during the course of our day and honor Him in our actions, behavior, and attitude, He responds as the loving Father He is.

Certainly the Father who loves us, the Savior who gave His life for us, and the Holy Spirit who lives inside us deserve our homage and our allegiance. If we're too busy to commune with God regularly and days go by without our even thinking of Him, we're doing Him and ourselves a great disservice. That's right. We're also hurting ourselves—denying ourselves the strength, wisdom, courage, and companionship that could be ours through the One who loves us most. To deny ourselves times of receiving rest, peace, guidance, and comfort from God is to deny our souls the *maintenance* they require.

Spending time with the Lord and nurturing the spiritual part of me didn't come naturally. It took quite a while for me to develop a way to pray and meditate and rest in God that works for me. And I'm constantly finding ways to improve what I'm doing. I'm nowhere near where I want to be, but I'm getting there. I so identify with the apostle Paul when he wrote:

> I do not consider myself to have "arrived," spiritually, nor do I consider myself already perfect. But I keep going on, grasping ever more firmly that purpose for which Christ grasped me...I do not consider myself to have fully grasped it even now. But I do concentrate on this: I leave the past behind and with hands outstretched to whatever lies ahead I go straight for the goal—my reward the honour of being called by God in Christ (Philippians 3:12-14 PHILLIPS).

Maybe it will inspire you to prayer and time with God if I invite you to step back in time with me to my teenage years. That's when I first discovered God loves me and longs for my company.

My New Beginning

When I was 16 one of the families in the church I attended Sunday mornings invited me to come to a Friday evening youth meeting. I'd never been to any kind of evening service before then. Anxious for an opportunity to get out of the house, I asked my mother and she said I could go.

That Friday night the young man speaking said that in every human being there is a void, a space, a vacant area that can only be filled by God through Jesus Christ, His Son. And he also talked about allowing the God of the universe to become the Lord of our lives. I made a commitment to serve the God of the universe for the remaining days of my life and to make Him my Lord. And a miraculous thing happened! The void that I didn't even understand before I went there—didn't even know existed until I went that Friday evening—was filled.

With love.

With peace.

With a sense of companionship I'd never experienced. Accepting Christ was right for me then, and living for Him is still right for me now. I'm in awe about how God chose to do that in my life. (I don't remember the name of that young man who taught that night, but I look forward to seeing him in heaven!)

What happened following that decision was something I hold near and dear to my heart because I believe it was the beginning of my journey, my search, my continual study in the area of prayer. Three married couples came up to me that night. It was a small church, and these three couples were teams who worked with the youth ministry and taught Sunday school. They hugged me, looked me straight in the eyes, and said, "Donna, we've been praying for you for eight years!" A rush of emotion covers me every time I think of those words.

I didn't understand the complete magnitude of that incident, but I was deeply touched with the realization that I—a skinny, big-nosed, little Italian kid who rode the Sunday school bus every Sunday morning, whose parents had not darkened the doors of the church in years, who did not contribute financially to the church—was important enough in their eyes to merit *eight years* of faithful prayer. Their fervent desire was that I would come to know Jesus as my Savior. I look back on that night and relish those words and that dedication. I count it as a privilege that those people cared for me.

That was the beginning of a personal odyssey. I began to ask questions about prayer…its purpose, its magnitude, and its effects on human lives. I want to share with you a few things I've learned over the years.

Prayerful Decisions

Now I know if I were to ask you if you already have a prayer life, and you were honest, you most probably would admit you don't. How do I know? From experience. I've talked with hundreds of women through the years, one-on-one, who have cried and said to me, "I want to pray. I know the Word tells me I should pray. But I don't know how I can get to it. Right now I'm lucky if I can spend five minutes a week praying. I want to have more time to pray."

Let me classify one way to look at prayer with two simple terms: *formal prayer* and *informal prayer*. God's Word tells us we should pray without ceasing (1 Thessalonians 5:17), and those are what I call informal prayers. These are the prayers that we say in the regular course of our day. For example, as we walk into the grocery store at eleven o'clock and we think of our child who's taking an exam just then, and we say, "Lord, help Scotty keep the names and dates straight for his history test." Or as we drive down the street we see an automobile accident and say, "God, provide strength to the people involved in that accident. Keep them from permanent harm and prepare their souls for salvation." Or as we drive children to school in the carpool we offer a prayer of protection and strength for them as they pile out of the car.

Informal prayers help keep us in a sanctuary frame of mind, and that attitude is an essential part of our lives. Think of it as a running conversation through the course of a day. God is always here, always listening, always loving, and always interested in every detail of our lives. I can't explain how such a wonderful thing can be true; it simply is—and I accept that reality by faith.

God wants *connection* with you, even if it's a quick thought of Him, a simple word of thanks, a cry for help in a moment of trouble or pain.

Formal prayer is when we deliberately set aside time for prayer. Jesus is our example for this. In the gospels, we're told, "And rising very early in the morning, while it was still dark, he departed and went out to a desolate place, and there he prayed" (Mark 1:35). Jesus had a time and He had a place to meet His Father. Two other things to note: He made this time in prayer a high priority, putting it first in His day before anything else, and He looked for a place where He could be alone and uninterrupted. Did He find it? Yes…but only for a time. Scripture goes on to tell us, "Simon and those who were with him searched for him, and they found him and said to him, 'Everyone is looking for you.' And he said to them, 'Let us go on to the next towns, that I may preach there also, for that is why I came out'" (Mark 1:36-39).

I smile as I read these words. The disciples were like kids who can't stand to let their moms have a minute or two alone. They actually went out searching for Jesus, saw that He was deep in prayer, and promptly went over to interrupt Him: "Hey, don't You know there are some needs out there? People are asking for You. What are You doing out here by Yourself?"

The Bible doesn't say whether Jesus sighed at this point, but I can certainly imagine one as He basically responded, "Okay, okay. Let's get back to work. Let's get back into our regular routine."

Jesus longed for opportunities to spend time alone with His Father. They were more important to Him than eating and sleeping. We're also told, "One day soon afterward Jesus went up on a mountain to pray, and he prayed to God all night. At daybreak he called together all of his disciples" (Luke 6:12 NLT). Though Jesus lived in constant communion with the Father, He made sure He set aside time to get alone and pray.

As I said earlier, I know many of you reading this book do not, at present, have a special time set aside for formal prayer. For a long time I didn't either. In fact, I spent the first 10 years of my Christian life struggling, trying to get a handle on prayer. The church I was part of didn't teach accountability in areas such as this. Many churches at that time said, "Good job. Well done. You're a Christian now. You're in the church. You're on your way to heaven. So get on with living."

And I did that. I got immediately involved in *doing*. I never learned about "being" with God. Nevertheless, I had, like all believers, an innate desire to commune with God. I truly wanted a relationship with Him. I just didn't know how to go about it.

As a young woman eager to serve the Lord, I paid close attention to the older ladies in my church. I wanted to be like them. But after a while I thought I'd never make it. I was blown away when one woman remarked at a prayer meeting, "I spent an hour with the Lord this morning."

An hour? I thought. *An hour! Amazing! How does she do it? I can't even read my Bible's table of contents without yawning. What's her system? And what is wrong with me?* I went home after hearing that comment with a big load of guilt on my back. I thought, *She spent an hour with the Lord this morning, and I couldn't manage five minutes. God must be really disappointed in me.*

The very next morning I decided I too was going to start my day by spending an hour with the Lord. I was living in my mother's three-room apartment and had my own bedroom. First I made my bed. Then I got ready. I looked at my little clock radio, and it read eight o'clock. At that point the only prayer position I knew was on my knees. So I reverently got down and began my hour of prayer. I offered a "Thank You, Lord" for my mother, my father, my brother, my school, and my church. I listed my friends, and then I asked for God's help and protection in my life. And then…I was done. I had nothing left to say.

I thought I'd prayed a long time, but when I looked up at the clock it was 8:04. I had just prayed for everything in the universe that I knew to pray for in four minutes. Talk about disappointment! In my memory, I kept hearing the words of that lady who'd spent an hour with the Lord Sunday morning. I had thought—hoped—wanted to do the same. But with no direction, no plan, and no preparation, I couldn't do it.

Why am I sharing this story? Because it may be that you too have been intimidated by the remarks of an older believer or an excited Christian talking about his or her hours of talking to God. Please let me set the record straight. If you're a believer and have made Jesus Christ your Savior and Lord, there are *no* specifications or standards to adhere to regarding having conversations with your heavenly Father... except sincerity.

I encourage you to begin slowly with prayer and Bible study. Set aside 10 minutes a day at first or even 15 minutes a week. (Remember, this is a starting point. You'll increase the time as you settle into your routine and enjoy your time with God.) This exercise is like all others—it builds and becomes easier as you do it. Enjoy your practice as you give God attention and space—and give yourself grace. Try a variety of practices and see what works the best for you. Read the Word first. I've found it very helpful to start with a psalm or proverb. If you don't have a specific plan for your prayer time, try reading a proverb daily. You'll commune with God and become more prudent and wise. Then sit quietly and listen. This may feel uncomfortable at first, but the time and waiting will soon become a blessing.

When beginning a prayer-time commitment, don't go for huge leaps. Instead, go for baby steps. Progress will lead to more progress, and before long your life is being changed by your regular, set-aside time with God.

Please know God loves you more than you can even begin to understand. You delight His heart *anytime* you say, "My Father" and continue talking to Him. He's not holding a stopwatch over your head as you kneel...or sit...or lie down...or stand...or walk to pray. He's not frowning or disappointed in you when your mind wanders or you find a day has gone by without taking time to seek Him in a formal way.

God doesn't carry around a big ledger to mark when you pray at the same time in the same place every day.

No, God wants a *love* relationship with you. He wants to fill every empty place in your heart. He wants to meet every named and nameless longing. He wants to shoulder your burdens, carry your hurts, soothe your perplexities, and heal your deepest wounds from the inside out.

Simon Peter may have been a rough, tough fisherman with bulging muscles and calloused hands, but he had hurts and sorrows too. And he knew right where to take them. He wrote to a group of believers, "You can throw the whole weight of your anxieties upon him, for you are his personal concern" (1 Peter 5:7 PHILLIPS).

So start small in your formal prayer time if you have to. Do what you can, and don't be bullied by the talk, testimony, or claim of someone else. Focus on *your* relationship with God.

Just Do It!

Are you familiar with a Christian author named Evelyn Christianson? She wrote a very inspiring book called *What Happens When Women Pray*. I had the privilege of spending time with Evelyn at a luncheon. I remember thinking, *Oh boy! Here's my chance. I've got Evelyn Christianson right across the table from me.* Nobody else was there, and we had unlimited time. In that moment, I determined that

---

From Emilie

Many women ask, "How can I spend an entire hour praying?" I created a "prayer basket" (see "Ask, Seek, Knock...and Never Stop!" chapter). I keep my Bible and supplies in it so I'm quickly ready to spend time with the Lord. And do you know what? After an hour I don't want to stop. You'll be amazed at how the spirit of God will settle your mind and help you focus on Him.

I would find out the secrets of effective prayer from the prayer warrior of prayer warriors.

When the time was right, after a certain amount of small talk, I cleared my throat and asked her the big question that was on my mind: "Evelyn, tell me, what will really help my prayer life? And what can I share with women as I teach on this subject?"

I'm not sure what I expected. Maybe I thought she would gaze off into celestial places and answer me in a well-modulated, super-spiritual voice. But that's not what happened. Not at all.

She looked up, smiled, and said, "Oh, that's easy: *Do it!*"

"Oh," I replied, a bit taken aback. "Well, I know *that*. But what I meant was, What can you tell me that I can share with other women to inspire them?"

She looked at me very seriously. "Donna, if I could condense everything I've ever written or spoken about on the subject of prayer into two words, I would say, *'Do it!'*"

And in all the years since that meeting with Evelyn, I've never found better advice.

My great desire is for you to understand the wonder of a prayer life so you'll be inspired to begin. If you've never cultivated an informal prayer life, carrying on a running conversation with the Lord through your day, start. Shoot short little "arrow prayers" toward heaven.

> Good morning, Lord.
>
> Give me strength today, Father.
>
> Help me to really listen to my daughter today as she seeks my attention.
>
> Have mercy on me.
>
> Show me how to better love my husband.
>
> What a beautiful morning, Lord. Thank You for the way You made the dew sparkle on the grass.
>
> Please help me with this call I have to make.
>
> You know I'm in a hurry, Lord. Please help me find a parking place.

There are many helpful books on the market that can give you much more help and many more practical details on prayer. The experienced prayer warrior authors can give you the *what*, the *why*, the *where*, the *when*, and the *how* of prayer.[1] Also talk to people you know who pray. Ask them about their experiences and what they do and don't do.

Remember that prayer isn't a duty—it's a privilege and a delight. You have an all-wise, all-powerful God who loved you before you were even conceived. He wants to hear from you. He wants to hear the secrets of your heart, wants to help you through all the ups and downs of your day, wants to hear your concerns, wants to forgive your sins, and wants to give you the strength to be the younique woman of God He created you to be. He wants you to hear from Him, to gain in wisdom and insights. Talk to God…and make sure you *listen!*

Attaching Your Children to God's Word

Kay

He knew his time was short. The apostle Paul was well aware that he would soon face beheading by the Romans because of the gospel of Jesus Christ. Knowing these things, he did just what you and I might have done in the same circumstance. He sat down and wrote a letter to one of the dearest people in his life—Timothy, his son in the faith and his companion through many trials and tribulations.

Faith Under Pressure

Paul became acquainted with Timothy on one of his missionary journeys. This young man's hometown was Lystra, a Roman colony in the province of Lycaonia, in Asia Minor. Scripture tells us that Timothy was "the son of a Jewish woman who was a believer, but his father was a Greek, and he was well spoken of by the brethren who were in Lystra and Iconium" (Acts 16:1-2). There was something about this devout young man that captured the apostle's attention, and Paul invited him along on a journey.

Now many miles and some 18 years later, as Paul faced his last days in a dreary Roman dungeon, he wrote to the young man who had been such a help and encouragement to his ministry. And in the midst of that letter, the veteran missionary laid down a stern warning.

> But realize this, that in the last days difficult times will come. For men will be lovers of self, lovers of money, boastful, arrogant, revilers, disobedient to parents, ungrateful, unholy, unloving, irreconcilable, malicious gossips, without self-control, brutal, haters of good, treacherous, reckless, conceited, lovers of pleasure rather than lovers of God, holding to a form of godliness, although they have denied its power; avoid such men as these (2 Timothy 3:1-5).

Difficult as times had been for believers, life was going to get worse. Much worse. And Paul wanted his young disciple to be ready for what was coming. Then, just a few lines later in that letter, he went on to say, "Now you followed my teaching, conduct, purpose, faith, patience, love, perseverance, persecutions, and sufferings, such as happened to me at Antioch, at Iconium and at Lystra; what persecutions I endured, and out of them all the Lord rescued me!" (verses 10-11). Paul was saying, "When the pressure's on, my son, when the going gets really rough and you don't know where to turn, remember what I taught you and model what you've seen in my life."

Can you say the same thing to your children if you knew they were facing great trials and hardships? (And they certainly will.) Can you say words like these?

> Johnny, Susie, I want you to remember what Mommy and Daddy taught you from God's Word. Remember the precepts we passed on to you and the verses you memorized. Remember what we taught you about how to discover truth for yourself. Use what we studied in the Bible together—what you learned about God and how He is sovereign. Look at what people are to do when things aren't easy. Remember how the Lord has helped us time and again.

If Paul prophesied that the days immediately following his death would be difficult for believers, how much more difficult will it be for our children and grandchildren? We face very trying times in the days ahead. Although the persecution of believers is more subtle in our society, it's certainly going to get worse as we approach the time of our Lord's return. Add to that the tidal-wave onslaught of a sensual, godless culture, and parents have great reason to be concerned…just as Paul was for Timothy.

Paul goes on to his young friend:

> But evil men and impostors will proceed from bad to worse, deceiving and being deceived. You, however, continue in the things you have learned and become convinced of, knowing from whom you have learned them, and that from childhood you have known the sacred writings which are able to give you the wisdom that leads to salvation through faith which is in Christ Jesus (verses 13-15).

"Deceiving and being deceived." That's a picture of our twenty-first-century world. And the deceit is everywhere! It permeates our culture—from the Internet to TV, from movies to magazines, from news broadcasts to education, from entertainment to organized religion. And as Paul said so clearly, it proceeds "from bad to worse."

I read recently that even in evangelical Christianity circles only seven percent of people hold a biblical worldview. A biblical worldview means processing and analyzing everything that happens in the world and in life through the lens of God's eternal Word. It's not your opinion or the news commentator's opinion or some celebrity's opinion that counts. What counts are the truths and precepts of God's unchanging Word.

From Donna

With each of my grandchildren I chose a special verse to whisper in their ears from the day they were born. Every time I see them I say, "Let me whisper in your ear," and then I quote the verse.

Are you preparing your children for the pressures and temptations of a world completely opposed to Christ and the standards of the Bible? Or are they being raised on a steady diet of TV, the Internet, the amoral and nongender agenda being promoted in public schools? That, precious daughters, is what this brief chapter is all about.

Vital Attachments

Can you picture Paul down in that filthy, horrible dungeon, quill pen in hand, pausing a moment before he inscribes ink on parchment? Thinking of the "young son in the Lord" he loved and valued so much, Paul pours his heart into this last letter. He writes, "You, however, continue in the things you have learned and become convinced of, knowing from whom you have learned them" (verse 14).

In God's plan, Timothy was attached to the apostle Paul. The older man spent time with him, taught him, and discipled him. Now in this crucial hour, with death looming before him, Paul wanted to make sure Timothy was also firmly attached to Jesus Christ.

The goal of a mother (and father) is very much the same. Your initial objective is to attach your children to yourself. They need physical attachment, emotional attachment, and spiritual attachment. Your ultimate goal as a parent, however, is to draw your children to Christ in you so they'll choose to become attached to the Lord Jesus when they get older. Then, no matter what happens to you in the days to come, your children will be linked to their loving, all-knowing, all-powerful Savior. When it comes time for you to pass from this earth, you can say to your kids, "Continue in the things you have learned and become convinced of...from childhood you have known the sacred writings which are able to give you the wisdom that leads to salvation through faith which is in Christ Jesus."

Those "sacred writings" are between the two covers of your Bible. And the reason the world is impacting the church today, rather than the other way around, is because we have departed from the Word. We may occasionally read what other men and women have written *about* the Bible, but we aren't reading and studying the Bible—the very words of God—enough.

God-Breathed

Real Bible study requires time. It's not difficult; it simply takes an investment of energy, thought, and prayer. Many people want something quick and easy—a quick hit like a jolt from a double espresso.

But our Teacher, the Holy Spirit, works best when we give Him time to gently weave His threads of truth through our thoughts and hearts. True Bible study, such as the inductive studies we teach at Precept Ministries, brings you face-to-face with truth—not what you believe or I believe, but what the Word of God actually says.

Paul reminded Timothy that "all Scripture is inspired of God." When we say the word *inspired,* we think of feeling challenged or motivated. But the Greek term translated *inspired* really means *God-breathed.* It is truth from God's very mouth. He breathed it, and it is "profitable for teaching."

From Emilie

After a seminar an Amish mother told me her five children learned to read using the Bible. Think how those children must have God's Word written on their hearts. They may choose to go down their own way, but they'll know the way home.

You and your husband are the primary teachers of your children, and the Bible is your primary and all-important text from which you teach. If your sons and daughters are going to learn about God and His ways, it will be because you've invested your life into teaching them how to study God's Word. If they don't know the Bible and don't know God, you can't blame the Sunday school teachers or the church. It's not their primary job. It's *your* job as a parent.

Remember what Moses said? "These words, which I am commanding you today, shall be on your heart. You shall teach them diligently to your sons and shall talk of them when you sit in your house and when you walk by the way and when you lie down and when you rise up" (Deuteronomy 6:6-7).

When you read this passage carefully you'll see God is speaking of two different kinds of instruction. First there is the formal and structured teaching. The parents are "to teach them diligently." Children's minds are steel traps, far more capable of learning than we think they are. In earlier times parents were the primary teachers of their children.

At the ages of 12 to 14, these home-taught boys and girls had amassed so much learning they were attending and graduating from college while still in their teens.

Second, after the formal teaching, there was the "talking." I call it "reviewing and applying"—weaving the Scriptures into the fabric of everyday life. This means teaching your children to view all of life in the light of Truth—the unchanging, inerrant Word of God.

God instructed the Israelites to so hold to the Word of God in their minds and hearts that they would naturally pass it along to their children. They were to talk about it in the morning at the breakfast table and talk about it before bedtime at night. They were to teach and reflect out loud on God's precepts as they sat together in their houses on a winter night and as they went for family walks in the springtime.

In these natural, unstructured settings the reality of a holy God and His good ways becomes intertwined with everyday living—just as it should be. Children feel free to ask questions and wonder about things out loud, knowing their thoughts will be taken seriously and that their parents love to talk about God and His Word.

From Donna

No one knows and applies the discipline of Scripture study better than Kay. How exciting to take her direction and make it come alive in the heart of your family for God's glory! That's her message— listening to the Spirit of God and implanting a love of His Word in the next generation.

How I wish I'd started this when my daughter was young.

This Book, this Bible, precious one, is God's attachment to you. This is God! God's heart…God's eyes…God's hands…and God's thoughts toward you. And the more you link your life to its truths, the more your children will follow that pattern.

Perhaps you've read about Bob and Emilie and their long ordeal with Emilie's cancer. It was an arduous, extremely painful process that was emotionally, spiritually, and physically draining. How did they get through it? How did they hold together as a family? How did they continue to help and minister to others even in their darkest days in the deepest valleys? They survived because they were already attached to God's Word and His promises. They simply continued to live as they always lived, drawing strength from their relationship with God and bringing others—especially their own family—into that attachment.

This desire to be pleasing to the One to whom we owe our lives is also what has gotten Jack and me through horrendous trials of our own.

Not by Bread Alone

A few pages beyond the Deuteronomy passage we just looked at, Moses gave God's people a little perspective as they were about to enter the Promised Land.

> All the commandments that I am commanding you today you shall be careful to do, that you may live and multiply, and go in and possess the land which the LORD swore to give to your forefathers. You shall remember all the way[s] which the LORD your God has led you in the wilderness these forty years, that He might humble you, testing you, to know what was in your heart, whether you would keep His commandments or not. He humbled you and let you be hungry, and fed you with manna which you did not know, nor did your fathers know, that He might make you understand that man does not live by bread alone, but man lives by everything that proceeds out of the mouth of the LORD (Deuteronomy 8:1-3).

In essence God is saying, "For 40 years I've been attaching Myself to you, proving that I can take care of you. For 40 years I've brought water out of the rocks for you and your flocks to drink. I've put manna on the ground—the very bread of angels—every morning with the dew. I brought you quail to eat when you thought there was no meat for a thousand miles. I led you by a cloud all day long and gave light to your camp with a pillar of fire at night. I put the fear of you into your enemies and kept them from harming you. I even kept your shoes from wearing out! Don't you see how I've attached you to Myself for your good and your blessing?"

Through all those years Israel didn't need grain or flour or ovens for baking bread. Why? Because God supplied their bread—honeysweet and nutty-flavored—so they'd see and understand that He was all they needed. And after they were finally in the Promised Land and harvesting grain and baking their own bread, He wanted them to remember that He was the ultimate Provider and could take care of their every need.

Your children need to know that about God too. As they watch you make the Lord your everything, your all-in-all...as they watch you give God's Word a central, honored role in your home and your family, they too will learn to attach themselves to the Lord. They too will build their lives on the security of Hebrews 13:5-6: "Make sure that your character is free from the love of money, being content with what you have; for He Himself has said, 'I WILL NEVER DESERT YOU, NOR WILL I EVER FORSAKE YOU,' so that we confidently say, 'THE LORD IS MY HELPER, I WILL NOT BE AFRAID. WHAT WILL MAN DO TO ME?'"

The single most important thing in all of life is to be attached to the Lord! He will be your children's help, their strength, their companion, their courage, and their provision through all their lives—no matter what circumstances or trials they face and even long after you've passed from the scene. It breaks my heart to see so many young people today who have no attachment to God or His Word.

- They don't understand God created them, just as He did the world, and He has a purpose for their lives.
- They don't understand there is a God who loves them.
- They don't understand there is a Savior who died for them, and His name is Jesus Christ.

- They don't understand they have Truth itself embodied in a Book that will guide them step-by-step through every problem and challenge of life.

- They don't understand they could have a covenant Friend who will never be untrue and a Helper who will never leave their sides.

- They don't understand they are so attached to God that their bodies—every part!—belong to God and are to be used to honor God.

And why don't they understand these things? Because their mothers and fathers never took the time to lead them by word and example into an eternal attachment with the living God.

Beloved, you can be the person who leads your children into abundant life in Christ. As you give top priority to your relationship with the Lord—daily studying His commands and precepts—as you attach yourself to Him more and more every day, your sons and daughters will see what it means to walk with God. As I write this I'm reminded of a story one young mother who is a Precept student told me. She wanted her children to see how she marked her Bible as she studied, so she would get on the bed and read to them from her Bible, showing them how she used a cross to mark "Jesus" so she wouldn't miss anything God said about Him. Her one concern, however, was that one of the children would get hold of her Bible and do their own markings! So she taught them that picking up Momma's Bible was expressly forbidden and carried with it certain punishment.

One day, to this mother's horror, she came out of the shower and found her daughter on the floor with the "forbidden" Bible open and her not-so-clean finger moving over those sacred marked pages. As my friend opened her mouth to chasten her child, she immediately closed it when her daughter looked up in pure delight and said with her little finger on the page, "Look, Momma! Jesus is all over the Bible!"

How I would love to introduce you to all the children who grew up studying the Bible inductively with their mothers and dads. The young ones who did Precept courses even before they were teen-agers, sitting in classes with their parents. I wish you could see what fine adults they've become, what loving husbands and wives...and parents! I've lived long enough to see the second and third generation of "Precepters." And to many of them I'm still "Pretty Aunt Kay." (I brainwashed them in this regard as they grew up and came to studies, conferences, and our student "Boot Camps." However, they did learn mighty truths about God!)

"So how do I share Christ specifically?" you ask. O precious one, I understand. I didn't know how either until I was in my thirties. Precept Ministries can show you and teach you how. This is God's calling upon my life and the lives of the men and women who serve at Precept. You can learn online, in person, or through the mail. Wherever you live across this nation or around the world, we'll help you. We're in 150 countries and our materials are in nearly 70 languages. Just contact us at Precept.org. We have inductive studies for children (*Dicover 4 Yourself,* as I mentioned earlier), students of all ages, and men and women at all different levels of commitment and time availability. (For more information, see the back of this book.)

From Donna

Attaching the Word to your children's hearts can never start too early. Read the Word aloud during your pregnancy.

Yes, it's true that even after all our careful teaching, some of our children may choose to go their own way in spite of our example. But at least you'll be giving them the opportunity to clearly see the path of life and understand what they'll lose if they walk away from Jesus and what He offers. And when they've become wearied and bruised and battered by the consequences of their worldly lifestyles, whether they take it or not, they'll know the way home.

Ask, Seek, Knock...
and Never Stop!

Emilie

Hurry, hurry, hurry.

Faster, faster, faster.

I'm always on the go, and you probably are too. Technology, marvelous as it may be, hasn't done a thing to ease our pace. In fact, it has pushed us harder and faster. The faster I move, the more someone wants and expects me to take it up yet another notch. I'm certain this is not what God had in mind when He created us. As His children we need to fight the urge to be swept along in this hurry-up mentality.

So what's the alternative? Becoming castaways on a tropical island? Getting rid of our computers and cell phones? No, if we're to function effectively, we must find a healthy balance. Living in hyperdrive may not be God's will, but neither is checking out of life and collecting cobwebs. I remember reading something Chuck Swindoll said years ago: "The zealot says, 'I would rather burn out than rust out!' But what's the difference? Either way you're out!"

Again, there must be balance, a *moderation* (my family's favorite word). In order to accomplish this equilibrium I've learned to pray on my feet or—to say it another way—to pray on the go.

Ask, Seek, Knock

From one end to the other, Scripture gives us examples of where and how to pray:

- "Pray without ceasing" (1 Thessalonians 5:17).

- "Call upon Me in the day of trouble; I shall rescue you" (Psalm 50:15).

- "Pour out your heart before Him; God is a refuge for us" (62:8).

- "Seek the LORD while He may be found; call upon Him while He is near" (Isaiah 55:6).

- "Ask, and it will be given you; seek, and you will find; knock, and it will be opened to you" (Matthew 7:7).

One of the main purposes of faith is to bring us into direct, personal, vital contact with the living God. When we pray, we admit our profound need, our helplessness to do life without Him. Even though God knows all of our daily needs, our praying for them changes our attitude from complaints and criticism to praise. In some real-but-mysterious way, praying allows us to participate in God's personal plan for our lives.

Jesus taught His disciples that "at all times they ought to pray and not lose heart" (Luke 18:1). Even though answers to prayer don't always come along immediately, we should not be discouraged…or stop praying! Oh, how my family had to learn these things as we prayed fervently for God to heal my cancer and all that goes with being a cancer patient. We wanted an immediate healing that would have the medical profession declaring, "It's a miracle!" Instead we had to learn time and again that God's timetable was not our own.

Trust Him for Everything

Why are some people healed and others not? Why do some get miracles while others pray just as hard and every bit as sincerely but remain ill or even die from disease? After endless months and years of petitioning God, I've come to realize that "God's will" *will* be done.

And His will is good.

He has a perfect plan and timetable for each of us. The sooner we recognize this in our Christian walks the quicker we'll understand that His thoughts are greater than our thoughts and His ways are greater than our ways.

Yes, God healed me of my mantle cell lymphoma, and I give Him praise for that. From the very beginning I claimed John 11:4 as my theme verse: "This sickness is not to end in death, but for the glory of God, so that the Son of God may be glorified by it."

What amazing peace I received when I turned this dramatic situation over to God. Bob and I agreed that through this valley God was going to be glorified. That declaration grew out of years and years of previous prayers and diligent study of God's Word and His promises. We came to understand—and prove—that we could trust God for everything. Yes, even for our very lives. With David we learned to say, "But as for me, I trust in You, O LORD, I say, 'You are my God.' My times are in Your hand" (Psalm 31:14-15).

No matter how circumstances appeared on the surface, we were convinced God was working out all things for His glory and our personal interest. This kind of faith makes life so exciting. We don't have to search the world for the purpose of life; we've found it and live it daily. The Westminster Confession of Faith expresses our goal very clearly: "Man's chief end is to glorify God and enjoy Him forever." Prayer helps us establish this purpose in a profound and deeply personal way. Without the wondrous gift of prayer, how could we ever gain the sense that our lives on earth have meaning?

We couldn't. We would be in that lost and desolate state described by the apostle Paul: "Without hope and without God in the world" (Ephesians 2:12 NIV). We essentially have two choices. We can pray or we can lose heart (Luke 18:1). You and I can live lives marked by faith and hope or we can surrender to lives filled with fear, anxiety, worry, and despair. Give praise to God because we have His strong arms around us! We cry out to Him because—in Jesus—He calls out to us. When life seems overwhelming, God wants us to lift our hands to Him as His little children, wanting to be held in His loving arms. We may not even know what's wrong or why we feel heavyhearted or afraid. And we don't have to know. All we really need to know is where to turn.

When we face the many pressures of life there is only one effective, successful way "through it all"—we are to pray. Prayer is our way to the place of power, our path to the solutions for life's indecipherable dilemmas. Unbearable pressures need not be withstood by us when God's strong and willing shoulders are ready to bear them.

> Cast your burden upon the LORD and He will sustain you; He will never allow the righteous to be shaken (Psalm 55:22).

> Cast all your anxiety on him because he cares for you (1 Peter 5:7 NIV).

Prayer is crying out to a God, whom we can't see but can totally rely upon—a Father with tender compassion and a willingness to act on our behalf. Prayer always stirs the heart of God. Never doubt that, dear reader! Prayer always moves Him to act.

From Donna

God's constant communion and desire to direct us is the gift He sent to every believer when Jesus gave His life on the cross.

In the book of Romans, Paul reminds us that often we don't even know what to pray for or how to form the words (8:26). But God knows. Our Father knows when to answer in the particular way we asked and when it wouldn't be the best thing to do.

From our perspective the longed-for answer to our heartfelt prayers may indeed be long in coming, but there is no delay at all in an answer to the prayer itself. When we cry out to God there *is* an immediate answer. God rushes to our aid. The answer may be the squeeze of the Father's hand on ours, the quiet comfort of the Father's voice, or the simple reassurance of His presence amid the stresses and pressures still evident.

Why Do We Pray?

We pray to enter into an understanding of the Father's heart. While prayer may not always bring us a specific answer, it often brings us to the place where a direct answer is unnecessary to an understanding of God's will for our lives.

We can't establish a relationship with God apart from communicating with Him. Human desires and needs require communication. Prayer is an absolute necessity in the interchange of a believer's heart with the Father. But please understand this, my friend. Prayer may not look anything like the traditional picture—kneeling by a bedside with folded hands and soft light streaming through the window. In fact, one of the most effective prayers in all of Scripture took place on a dark night, on a wild sea, when Peter found himself sinking in the water instead of walking on it.

"Lord, save me!" he cried.

And Jesus did exactly that, gripping the panicked disciple's outstretched hand, pulling him out of the water, and guiding him back to the boat.

Prayer comes in many forms and in many ways, including—

- Sometimes when we're in motion, sometimes when we're still.

- Sometimes when the words come easily, and sometimes when we can't even speak.

- Sometimes on our knees, sometimes on our backs, sometimes on our feet, sometimes walking or running along a path.

- Sometimes when we're at leisure, sometimes when we're way behind schedule and in a frantic rush.

The place or position or situation doesn't really matter. What does matter is that we actually pray...and not just read about it or talk about it. The ideal? To "pray without ceasing," as the apostle Paul says.

Yes, I have truly learned how to pray on my feet and right in the middle of things. But whether I'm on my feet or on my knees, I want to be obedient to God's command to always be in an attitude of prayer.

Speed Dialing

Do you have God's private cell number? It's Jeremiah 33:3: "Call to Me and I will answer you, and I will tell you great and mighty things, which you do not know." God is always here, and we can always talk to Him. When we call, we're never put on hold. We never get a computerized angel voice telling us to press 1 and then press 4 and so on. We never get a recording or even a bored receptionist. We're directly connected to Him. If He had a desk, our call would ring at that desk. If He had a bedside, our call would ring at His bedside. And God answers the phone 24/7!

> In the morning, O LORD, You will hear my voice; in the morning I will order my prayer to You and eagerly watch (Psalm 5:3).

> When I remember You on my bed, I meditate on You in the night watches, for You have been my help, and in the shadow of Your wings I sing for joy (Psalm 63:6-7).

What an awesome God! He is always interested in the smallest details of our lives. There is nothing too trivial for Him. If it concerns us, it concerns Him. On our knees, on our feet, on the run…it doesn't matter. God is a Father who always has time for His kids.

A Morning Walk with God

For the past five years my goal has been to walk two to three miles every day. It takes me 30 to 40 minutes. Funny, isn't it, how we find time to do an aerobics class, work out, run, walk, or pursue other activities but somehow we "just can't find time" to pray. By necessity my time is well-planned each day. The majority of it is invested in preparing for seminars and speaking engagements. Add to those hours the letters to be answered, phone calls to return, the keeping of our home, loving Bob and my family, and my days are very full.

One of the messages I frequently bring to women is to do at least two things at a time. (Unlike many of our male counterparts, we women are natural multitaskers.) What follows is a big example of that in my own life.

My quiet time begins early each day with reading Scripture for 5 to 10 minutes. Then I flip open my prayer notebook to the correct day of the week and review those whom I will remember in prayer that day.

After my review of names and requests, off I go for my walk. From my first step out the door I adore and worship the Lord. Sometimes as I look around at the morning sky and the sunrise painting the clouds, I marvel at all He's done for me and given me. Often I'll find a praise song rising in my heart, and I may even lift my hands to worship as I walk. How grateful I am for my life, for my family and friends, for the amazing opportunities He gives me to reach and touch women's lives.

Then I begin the next phase of my "prayer walk"—confessing to God my failures, inadequacies, and other areas that I need to give over to Him. From there, I thank Him for His mighty forgiveness, His hands that always surround me with His love, and the way He carries me when I'm weak, tired, overwhelmed, downhearted, suffering, sick, sorrowful, or ashamed.

It's wonderful to let thankfulness and praise rise in my heart as I begin my day this way. It's like sweet water bubbling up from a mountain spring or a flower opening up to face the life-giving sunlight.

I'm thankful for the abundance I have. I'm thankful for you, my reader, reading these words at this very moment, whatever your circumstances and wherever in this world you might be. I'm thankful you possess a teachable spirit, a positive attitude, and are looking up to God's glory.

At the halfway point in my walk, I turn back toward home as I rejoice in His love and lay all my needs and requests at His feet. I ask the Lord to bring to my mind and heart the people and requests I reviewed before I began my walk. All the way home I pray for those dear people, bringing their needs before the Lord.

I remember the time when it dawned on me that I was spending almost an hour daily with Jesus. I got so excited about that! But maybe walking and praying don't appeal to you or isn't practical for you. Mary of Bethany loved to spend time sitting quietly at Jesus' feet, gazing up at His face, soaking in His every word. The important thing is to set a regular time to meet with Him and make it the top priority in your day.

From Kay

How I would love a prayer walk with Emilie. A Sabbath Day with Donna. I usually meet with God in a cozy place at home. I put my feet up, have my coffee cup within reach, supplies are handy, and I lay back on a pillow. I begin in God's Word. I read from one book of the Bible at a time...although sometimes I include a psalm. In my cozy place with God I remember nothing really matters but loving and pleasing Him.

I do, however, have strong biblical justification for "walking with God." The book of Genesis says that "Enoch walked with God; then he was no more, because God took him away" (Genesis 5:24 NIV). Apparently, God and Enoch walked so far and spent so much time together that one day God said to him, "Well, you've come this far, you might as well come on home with Me." And Enoch walked right off the planet and into heaven.

After Jesus died and was resurrected, two discouraged disciples were walking to a different town. Suddenly Jesus joined them on their trek. As they walked Jesus spoke at length with them and opened the Scriptures to them.

I encourage you to take a little time each day to be with Him. Ideally it should be around the same time of day. That will build a sense of expectancy in your heart as you anticipate meeting Him, worshiping Him, and receiving help and comfort from Him. That's the way it is for me. As I'm preparing to go for my walk—picking up my water bottle and tying my sneakers—I feel excitement building. I know when I step outside my front door Jesus is ready to head out. As much as I look forward to that time, I'm sure He looks forward to it even more.

Prayer Basket

If your prayer and devotional time is more like Mary of Bethany's than Enoch's, I want to share an idea for your daily appointment with God. And even if you do have an active regimen for prayer, putting together this prayer basket will help during those times when you stay in or find a few minutes for extra time with the Lord.

Keep the following items in a basket and take it with you to the place where you meet with Jesus regularly.

- a prayer notebook
- a pen
- a Bible
- a box of tissues for tears
- a small bunch of fresh or silk flowers to remind you of God's fragrance of love and the Holy Spirit who permeates your heart with joy
- a few cheery note cards so you can write words of encouragement to others

Keep your basket ready at all times with the organizational materials you need for your meetings with Jesus.

Remember, Jesus went to a mountaintop to pray. My "mountaintop" is the walk along a canal. Yours may be the closet, bathroom, kitchen table, bedroom, yard, rocker, car, a bench in the park on a lunch break, or your office at work.

Kay mentioned Susanna Wesley and her 19 children. Her "mountaintop" was a chair in the middle of her kitchen with an apron pulled over her head. All the Wesley kids knew that when Mom pulled that apron over her head she was meeting with God…and woe to the child who interrupted.

Wherever your place of appointment with the Lord might be, let your roots sink deeply into the soil of His wondrous love. He loves you so much He died for you, giving His life that you might receive eternal life by believing in Him, accepting Him, receiving Him.

For God so loved the world, that He gave His only begotten Son, that whoever believes in Him shall not perish, but have eternal life. For God did not send the Son into the world to judge the world, but that the world might be saved through Him (John 3:16-17).

These verses touched my heart when, as a 16-year-old Jewish girl, I first heard God's beautiful plan for my life. My Bob loved and cared for my life and my eternal soul. He shared with me his love for God the Father, God the Son, and God the Holy Spirit. During that momentous year of my life I had a monumental decision to make. I *did* love God and wanted to know Him better. I attended Hebrew school and had been confirmed in the synagogue. But when Bob shared with me Jesus as Messiah, he really made it clear that I had a need in my heart only Christ could fill. As I opened my heart to Jesus, the emptiness disappeared. Just like that!

I felt the comfort of His Spirit—like a warm blanket around my shoulders—and knew for the first time in my life that I would never be alone again. Almost immediately I found myself living the reality of the apostle Peter's words: "Like newborn babies, long for the pure milk of the word, so that by it you may grow in respect to salvation, if you have tasted the kindness of the Lord" (1 Peter 2:2-3). I *had* tasted the kindness of my newfound Lord, and I was hungry for His Word! Bob was excited to share with me and teach me, and I was excited to learn.

At 17 I proudly became Mrs. Bob Barnes. Many said our marriage would never last. But I knew in my heart it *could* work…as long as we both had the common goal of "seeking first the kingdom of God." Bob was teaching school and, to be honest, I was only four years older than his students. In fact, during my senior year in high school Bob signed my report cards!

Remembering to Pray

When I was 20, our Jenny was born, and when I was 21, we had 5 children under the age of 5! (We took in my brother's three children when their mother abandoned them, and our Brad came along shortly thereafter.) I don't think I could possibly have made it through this season of life without the infilling, undergirding grace and presence of God.

My life changed radically in those two years, and I could identify with David as he described God's help and encouragement in a time of great change and turmoil.

> The cords of death encompassed me
> And the terrors of Sheol came upon me;
> I found distress and sorrow.
> Then I called upon the name of the LORD:
> "O LORD, I beseech You, save my life!"
> Gracious is the LORD, and righteous;
> Yes, our God is compassionate…
> I was brought low, and He saved me.
> Return to your rest, O my soul,
> For the LORD has dealt bountifully with you
> (Psalm 116:3-7).

I'm still growing and learning. I've been on this lifelong walk with God for more than 52 years now, and I'm not finished yet. Nor is God finished with me. But what an exciting journey I'm on—and the same is probably true for you.

We've had our family crises and family sorrows—as I'm sure you've experienced as well. In times such as these, brothers and sisters in Christ have been a great source of strength and peace, praying for us when we simply couldn't pray for ourselves. If you have a friend in crisis, remember you don't have to "fix" everything or "solve" anything. That's God's job. Send a card or a note (so much more encouraging than an e-mail) or pick up the phone and say, "I care. I'm thinking about you. I will pray." Even if that is all you write, it will be enough.

From Donna

Never stop asking God for His plans in your life. Be open to change. When His plan doesn't match yours, smile and accept His direction.

Dear Jesus, may I never forget to say thank you to those who love and care for God, who pray for others in a world of 10,000 distractions. Help me reach out to them with Your love.

And may I never forget my unfailing Source of peace, joy, and healing. Thank You, Jesus, that You were there for this little Jewish girl and You're here for me now. Touch my heart for You. I want to serve and love You more each day...and may I never forget to pray!

Seven

If We Could Do
It All Again…

If I Could Do It All Again...
I Would Trust God More

Emilie

Doing something again is a nice thought, but none of us are granted do-overs in this life. Much as we may wish we could, we can't do it all again. As deeply as Kay, Donna, and I might like to go back to certain seasons of our lives or revisit certain attitudes or decisions we made in our younger years...we can't do it. No one can. God has placed each one of our lives on a timeline, with a specific beginning and a specific end. And wherever we may be on that line, going forward is our only option.

We can't go back, and we can't stand still.

We have to take life as it comes. Each new day brings a fresh opportunity to follow the Lord and—in His power and grace—begin life anew from this point forward. Praise His name! The Lord's mercies "are new every morning" (Lamentations 3:23).

So yesterday is yesterday and today is today, and life must be lived to the hilt in the 24 hours directly before us. Even so, here we are—Kay, Donna, and me—with the deep desire in our hearts to touch your life and the lives of other single women, wives, and mothers by pointing you toward wisdom we wish we'd possessed and practiced when we were younger.

A woman named Henrietta Mears was asked near the end of her

life, "What would you do differently if you could live your life over again?" Without hesitation she replied, "I would trust God more." Now if you knew the history of this remarkable woman, you would say she already trusted God in a deeply significant way. A Sunday school teacher at Hollywood Presbyterian for many years, Henrietta taught generations of young boys, many of whom went into fulltime ministry. She never married, and in the course of her long and fruitful ministry, Henrietta founded the Forest Home Christian Conference Center in Southern California and wrote a layman's overview of Scripture that is widely used to this day: *What the Bible Is All About*.

Toward the end of her life, however, looking back on all her opportunities and all she had accomplished for the Lord, Henrietta still said, "If I had it to do over again, I would trust God even more."

All three of us say the same thing. Each of us has seen miracles of provision, direction, empowerment, and healing in our walks with God through the years. Each of us has found the Lord to be completely faithful to His promises, blessing our lives above and beyond what we ever imagined.

Each of us trusts God.

But all of us wish we'd trusted Him even more.

A friend of mine in the state of Washington told me about walking along the mighty Columbia River early one morning. As he stopped on the trail to ponder the view, he noticed a little sparrow by the river's edge, dipping its tiny beak into the water. Then, having satisfied its thirst with a drop or two of the river, it flew away. My friend felt the Lord speak to him in that moment, "That's how much of My grace and power you are appropriating in your life. It's barely a drop of a mighty river."

No matter how much we trust the Lord, no matter how deeply we dip into His resources, there will always, always be more…infinitely more. We can't trust the Lord too much…and all of us trust Him too little.

Even though we look back now and wish we'd realized this more in our younger days, you can actually do something about it in your life now! As a woman, wife, and/or mother, place more of your trust and faith and confidence in God and in His Word. We promise, you'll never regret doing so!

At our Youniquely Woman conferences, a number of women have told us their marriages were saved because of what they learned. Perhaps, after reading this book, you too have made a decision to stay in a difficult marriage. You've decided to trust God for your marriage, for your mate—the man you fell in love with and to whom you have committed your life. You've decided to hang in there and trust God through a pressure-filled season of life. Your decision hasn't been easy, and maybe the road ahead doesn't look all that great. But you've made up your mind to trust God more. You will not regret that choice. Not now, not tomorrow, not forever.

If I Could Do It All Again...
I Would Be More Purposeful as a Parent

Kay

I once said in front of my adult children, "I wish I could go back and raise you again, knowing what I know now."

My son Mark said, "What's wrong with us the way we are?"

And of course I didn't mean there was anything wrong with them. I just wish that when Jack and I married, and in those early years of marriage with my first husband, Tom, we were more purposeful about raising our children.

In my book *Marriage Without Regrets* I suggest sitting down with your husband *before* you have children—or while they're still very young—and asking each other, "What do we want for them? What are the character values we want to see developed in their lives? What skills do we want them to have, to learn, and to know? What do we want them to understand about finances? What do they need to know about their sexuality and relating to the opposite sex—and when do they need to know it?"

These are such important, life-shaping concerns. And for the most part, I never thought to ask such things. I taught our boys some important things about how to take care of themselves and how to handle themselves in an emergency, but there were a number of all-important *life* questions I could have addressed as my sons grew up.

I wish we'd been more purposeful in that.

Learn from me, dear daughter. Think all this through, take it to the Lord, and then write it down and review it quarterly. Don't put it off. I know it may not seem so now, but the days of their childhood will soon be over. Believe me, time is fleeting and life is so very busy! It will be easy to forget it, to say, I'll do it later." Write yourself a reminder, put it on the front of the refrigerator or on the bathroom mirror, and don't remove it until this life-shaping task is done. You'll be so thankful you did—I promise!

If I Could Do It All Again...
I Would Spend More Time with My Children

Emilie

There were times as a mommy when I focused on mopping the floor or trying to make my house look perfect instead of sitting on that not-perfect floor and playing with my little ones. Looking back I wish I'd made time with my kids a bigger priority than my house.

The kitchen floor will always be there.

Church activities and commitments will always be there.

Professional and career opportunities may or may not always be there.

But it's a sure thing your small children will *not* always be there.

I really worked conscientiously and hard to be a good wife and mother. I wanted my meals to be perfect, my house to be perfect, and for everything to look "just so." There's nothing wrong with any of those goals, but I spent hours achieving them. I wish I'd invested a few more of those hours talking, singing, playing, teaching, walking, and laughing with my children—because the time with them as kids flew by so quickly.

It's interesting that when we talk to older women who are looking back on their lives, we almost never hear anyone say, "I wish I'd made more money" or "I wish I'd become president of that company."

But we do hear them say, "I wish I'd been there for my kids. I wish I'd valued those growing-up years more and spent more time with them."

Take steps today so this doesn't become one of your regrets.

If I Could Do It All Again...
I Would Treasure God's Word More

Donna

I remember as a young woman hearing some of the older ladies in my church talk about "the hope of heaven." At the time I really didn't know what they meant by that. I knew what hope was, and I thought I knew what heaven was, but I didn't understand the concept of "a hope of heaven." What did it mean? Was it just a nice-sounding phrase for elderly people? What did it imply for my daily life?

Looking back, I truly think God would have been happy to teach me more about that subject—and many other wonderful things—if I'd taken more time and made a more determined effort to seek Him through Bible study and prayer. I remember telling myself, "I'm just too busy. I'll pursue such things when I'm older and have more time." But the truth is that we all have the same amount of hours in a week, and we choose how to invest every one of them.

Before He left this earth, Jesus said to His disciples, "The Helper, the Holy Spirit, whom the Father will send in my name, he will teach you all things and bring to your remembrance all that I have said to you" (John 14:26). And of course that's true. The Holy Spirit is available to us 24/7, and His strong desire is to teach us the Word of God and help us understand and apply its truths. There will be times when that conversation will be very intimate, and He'll go beyond simply teaching us facts. He'll share His treasures with us! The book of Proverbs speaks of this heavenly wisdom in terms of precious rubies (Proverbs 8:11 NKJV). Just imagine a large, perfectly cut, multifaceted ruby catching and flashing the light from its deep-red heart.

It's a precious jewel.

It's a rare treasure.

I believe God wants to give us such treasures from His heart and from His Word. But most of us are too self-absorbed or running too fast through life to stop and receive His gifts of wisdom. He won't force His treasures on us or press them into our hands as we're running by Him in a frenzy.

The Holy Spirit reveals treasures of wisdom from God's Word when we take time to "ask, seek, and knock" and reserve a little corner of our day to read and study the Bible. I believe "the hope of heaven" was one of those valuable heirlooms of wisdom He wanted to share with me when I was younger, but I didn't take the time.

Sometimes, to be really honest, I was just too busy talking. And as we all know, you really can't talk and listen at the same time. I do wish I'd learned to listen more as a young woman…to listen to my co-workers, my friends (just listen for a change!), my family, and my Lord.

In later years I learned more about hearing God's voice through reading His Word. As I read, listened, and talked with godly women, a couple of phrases have stuck with me. First, I have sought to develop a "sanctuary frame of mind." To me that means I am quiet and still before God. That can happen when I'm alone with Him in a private place or when I'm in the middle of a hectic, busy day. God says to us, as He said to David, "Be still, and know that I am God" (Psalm 46:10). The New American Standard translation renders that verse: "Cease striving and know that I am God." In other words, discipline yourself to set aside the inner turmoil, the racing thoughts, the pressing worries, and all those big and small anxieties that gnaw at your peace and joy. Cease striving and realize that God is God, the all-powerful, all-knowing Being who loves you with everlasting love.

The second phrase I value is "a constant communion." Because God's Spirit has residence inside me, He wants to speak to me all the time. And when I get out of communion with Him, it's because I've ceased to listen or I've allowed other voices and noises to drown Him out, which essentially amounts to the same thing.

"A sanctuary state of mind" and "a constant communion" have become two credible, valuable, workable guidelines for me as I've walked with God over the last few years. I hope they help you too.

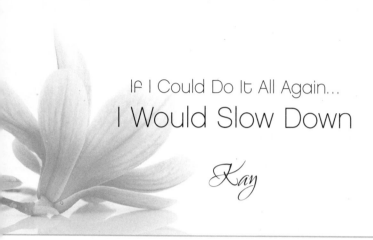

If I Could Do It All Again...
I Would Slow Down

Kay

IF I could redo my life, I'd slow down in two primary ways: first, in my speech and second, in the pace. The New Testament book of James, focused as it is on the practical outworking of faith in our lives, is one of those portions of Scripture that never fails to deliver conviction. Like a doctor probing for broken bones, James places his finger on life issues that often make me wince with recognition. In one particularly pointed statement, he tells us: "Everyone must be quick to hear, slow to speak and slow to anger" (James 1:19).

If I could do life over again, I would hold more closely to those words. As we all know, even though we may be forgiven by God and people, we can't "unsay" words carelessly spoken or uttered in frustration or impatience. Through the apostle James the Holy Spirit tells us to major on quiet listening and minor on talking and anger. Does that command go against the grain of our natural tendencies? Absolutely. And that's the point! God doesn't want us to live by our natural tendencies. He wants us to walk in the Spirit and live by the Word of God: "But I say, walk by the Spirit, and you will not carry out the desire of the flesh" (Galatians 5:16).

Years and years after the incident, my son Mark reminded me of a time when I'd spoken in anger to him. We were at home, and at that time we had two barns on the property. Although I can't recall any of the details, Mark apparently irritated me and I turned to him and said, "You are such a bother!"

I don't even remember saying that…but he remembers. And it's obviously stuck with him for years. He understands the situation a little bit better now because he has kids of his own. He loves me and he knows how very much I love him—it's been proven time and time again. Even so it amazes me to think how five careless words, spoken in a little outburst of irritation, lodged in his mind to remain for *decades*.

James says be slow to speak. Don't say the first thing that comes to your mind—especially if it's negative or critical. Take time to think through the situation and what you're going to say. If I could do it all again, I would choose my words carefully and speak graciously at all times. Remember when the good doctors took time to listen and then asked you to stick out your tongue and say "ah"? Let me share something I've done that has taught, convicted, and helped me in my speech. I've read through the book of Proverbs and colored in apple green *every* verse that has to do with the tongue. With those verses marked in my Bible it's easy to do a periodic diagnosis of how I'm using my words!

In a related issue, if I had the opportunity to go back and change things, I would also try to slow my sometimes-frantic life pace. I would stop trying to do too much, too fast. Have you ever seen a book—maybe an amateur-looking, self-published book—where the printing went right out to the edge of the page? You probably haven't seen many, because people don't like to read items that feel heavy and dense to the eyes. We prefer books with readable-sized print and nice margins because it's restful and inviting to the eye.

Some time ago I realized I've lived most of my life right up to the edge. There have been very few "margins"—open areas, white space, breathing room, or whatever you care to call it. At times this has made it difficult for people who work around me. Why? Because when I'm living and working up to the edge, that's where I want *them* to be too.

I want people to work at *my* pace...and sometimes it's hard to keep up with me! I make quick decisions and don't like to take time with a lot of details. I know I can make things happen faster if I don't have to explain what I'm doing or what I want someone else to do. Often it's easier to do it yourself, isn't it!

I've lived so much of my life in a hurry. I'm always trying to push more and more things into less and less time. The ministry God has given me (and Jack) is so huge! Precept Ministries International is in 150 countries and nearly 70 languages. I find myself flying all over the world because I long to meet with believers who have given everything, often at the risk of their freedom and lives, and are begging for more Precept studies because they are life-transforming. I've had a hard time learning to say no.

I have and had good reason to be busy, and I want to live before the Lord as someone who will be accountable for the time invested in this life. My life mission is terribly important to me. But then I look to Jesus. He, of course, had the most important mission of all. And though He never wasted time, He never seemed to be in a hurry either. Mission-driven as He may have been, He left room for margins in His earthly life. Sometimes it meant slipping away from everyone else and finding a remote place where He could think and pray. He said to His disciples on one occasion, "Come away by yourselves to a secluded place and rest a while" (Mark 6:31).

What He was saying was they needed a margin; they needed to slow down for a while to catch their breath and spend leisure time with their Lord. I've had a fair amount of such rest times in my life, and they've been priceless to me. But if I could do it all again, I would build in more. So pray for me, precious daughter in the Lord, that I'll learn my lessons and finish well in God's estimation. And I'll pray that for you too.

> I know that this will turn out for my deliverance through your prayers and the provision of the Spirit of Jesus Christ, according to my earnest expectation and hope, that I will not be put to shame in anything, but that with all boldness, Christ

will even now, as always, be exalted in my body, whether by life or by death. For to me, to live is Christ and to die is gain (Philippians 1:19-21).

Therefore we also have as our ambition, whether at home or absent, to be pleasing to Him (2 Corinthians 5:9).

You Can Do It!

Dear reader, have you noticed a pattern in our "If I could do it all again" responses? We're talking about giving priority to slowing down, listening, praying, meditating on the Word, and spending more time with our loved ones. Are you rolling your eyes a bit, thinking, *I'm already overwhelmed. Where will I find time to do all those things?* First of all, we're not insisting you make an immediate, radical change in lifestyle. We're talking about making changes by degrees... a step here, a step there, a little more of these priorities each day.

Second, the God we serve is the One who created time. No one understands the minutes and hours of our days better than He. And when we seek to honor Him and love our families more and more, He has a way of making everything up to us. He can bring us gifts of time when we least expect them. He'll also help us accomplish so much more than we can do on our own.

No, we can't do life over again. But we still have that amazing gift called *today!*

From Donna

Oh the fun Kay, Emilie, and I have when we meet! As sisters in the Lord who love each other and desire to communicate truth to women, we truly enjoy being together and sharing God's wisdom. It's like this chapter—a back and forth sharing about the faithfulness of God and the joy of being women. If I could do my life again, I would find Emilie and Kay in my twenties. I pray you have friendships like we do.

Eight

Continuing
the Adventure

Never Stop Growing

Donna

When Emilie, Kay, and I come to a town or city for a Youniquely Woman gathering, we're surrounded by hundreds of women we've never met before—and very likely will never meet again until heaven. But we don't feel like we're among strangers. Women understand one another. Our Creator has carefully constructed us and given us the ability and capacity to intuitively identify with each other and tune in to our emotions. Sometimes all it takes is a glance, a few words of conversation, a single tear, or a squeeze of the hand to sense what another woman is going through.

Perhaps you've heard your husband say at times, "How do you know all those things about her or about him? You've only just met." Men say that because it may take them a long, long time to know each other or to understand one another's hopes, dreams, and fears. In fact, they may *never* understand in that deep, more personal way women experience. And for most men, that's just fine with them.

But women are different.

Youniquely different.

Gloriously different.

Women talk about *life*. We talk about our relationships, the important people in our lives, and matters close to our hearts. That's why

I never feel out of place at my conferences and Youniquely Woman gatherings. To a large degree I know where you've been, where you're coming from, and what so deeply concerns you.

One of the things I know about you is your desire to grow, to reach higher, to achieve God's intent for you as one of His precious daughters.

The Desire Within

As I said, even if we've never met, I know you…at least some things about you. What do I know?

I know you're a woman created in the image of God.

You're probably married; you likely have children; and you care for "a place."

I believe at your core you want to do your best to follow where God leads.

And all of that means that somewhere in you—deep inside or right on the surface—you have a hunger to grow. You really want to be more than you are. You want to lay hold of your youniquely woman destiny. You want to experience more (and more and more still) of what God has for you now, in the midst of your present life, and in the days that remain for you.

That's what you want. Does it surprise you that God wants that for you too? It's a tenet in God's creation that every living thing either grows or dies. Nothing alive stays static; it's either going forward or slipping back. It's either reaching higher and higher for the sunlight or withering into itself.

Do you remember what Peter said about always growing? Here's how it reads in a popular paraphrase:

> So don't lose a minute in building on what you've been given, complementing your basic faith with good character, spiritual understanding, alert discipline, passionate patience, reverent wonder, warm friendliness, and generous love, each dimension fitting into and developing the others. *With these qualities active and growing in your lives, no grass will grow under your*

feet, no day will pass without its reward as you mature in your experience of our Master Jesus (2 Peter 1:5-8 MSG).

Active and growing! I love that. The God of all growing things has no intention of letting you stay where you are. He wants you to stretch, to learn new things, to live expectantly, to become more fruitful and productive, to nurture that secret, inner spot in your soul, and to make growth one of the priorities in your life. How do you do that? It's always a good idea to look ahead to the finished product—to think about what you want to grow into.

Have you considered what kind of middle-aged or older woman you want to be? Have you pondered how you would like to be remembered by others after you've left this earth? Doing so is an interesting exercise that can tell you a lot about yourself and help you make important choices now.

A Look Ahead

Do you want to be remembered as a woman of wisdom, a woman of energy and vigor, a woman who truly accomplished something for the Lord? Do you see yourself as a happy grandmother baking cookies with your grandchildren? Do you envision yourself as a gray-haired lady who wears bright colors and takes college courses? A weathered but wise woman who sips tea with her younger sisters and advises them? A gorgeous, well-kept, "not a gray hair on your head" woman who inspires others with her energy?

The first step in becoming this "fully grown" you of the future is visualizing the person you would love to be. Then ask, "Is this the person God is leading me to be? Is this the person I'm likely to become if I continue on my present path?"

The Gracious Woman

One key aspect to living for God is found in the word "gracious." Do you know that word? It means "someone full of tact, kindness, and politeness." Another definition is "someone displaying divine grace, mercy, and compassion." A truly unique, modern woman, the one we call "younique," is all of that, don't you think? It's one of the God-given ways we stand out from the crowd. Graciousness is how we treat others and how we represent our Lord.

I've learned so much about graciousness that I'd like to share with you! First, the gracious woman enjoys who she is. Do you know the song from the Broadway musical *Flower Drum Song* that goes "I enjoy being a girl"? You are who God created you to be. Don't fight it! If you're warm and caring to yourself, you'll also reflect that to others. Enjoy who you are—even if there are some things that need work and attention. After all, you are God's creation, and He doesn't make mistakes.

Here's a real test for graciousness: When you walk into a room full of people, what do you project to the crowd? Is it "Here I am!" or "There you are!" The gracious woman focuses on others. That's the kindness and politeness aspects of graciousness. Do you light up when others enter your world? If so, you are on the path to graciousness.

"Graciousness" also includes how we present ourselves. Now, you're listening to a girl who works really hard to present herself in an attractive way. I didn't have much to work with to begin with and age has taken its toll a bit, but I do all right in this area. Attractive is okay. When I talk with young women, they often tell me they feel pressure to look good, to focus exclusively on appearance. Looking your best is certainly good, but attractive is so much more than physical beauty. The most attractive women are the ones that have what I call "the basics" under control. They radiate confidence and kindness.

The "basics" are the things your mom told you (or should have):

1. *Take care of your appearance.* That means good hygiene every day. You tell your kids to do it, so do it yourself.

2. *Practice modesty.* Dress in the house and out on the town in a modest manner. It doesn't have to be ultra-conservative, but check your clothes choices. Do they draw undue attention to you or your body? Also, make sure your clothes are clean and

in good repair. Although "cleanliness is next to godliness" isn't in the Bible, it is a great principle.

3. *Know your style.* Attractiveness, even glamour, can be as simple as discovering what looks good on you and wearing it. For example, I wear black and white. Literally. If you walk into my closet, you'll see nothing but black and white clothes. Why? Black looks good on me. Plus, when I shop for bargains, I know when I find a delightful black sweater it will fit into my wardrobe. No worrying about dyeing shoes to match an outfit for me! Whatever your style, know it and stick to it.

4. *Watch your jewelry.* Many women wear too much jewelry. When I was just starting out in life, a wise, older woman told me that whenever I was going out to check my jewelry and then take one piece off before going out the door. When it comes to jewelry, less is better…and too much is not good.

5. *How you move and carry yourself.* Do you think this matters? It does! The gracious woman has good posture, gets out of a car with smoothness, and is relaxed rather than breathlessly rushed. Now if you have children you may say it's impossible to move graciously with an air of calm. But actually you can do it, even with the pressures of family life. It's really an attitude that translates into deliberate action. Practice being a woman whose actions show she is "fearfully and wonderfully made" as the Bible says. You are!

Maintain the basics and you'll radiate attractiveness. And don't fret. Developing graciousness may take time, so be patient.

> *Beauty without virtue is a flower without fragrance.*

Getting Honest

Looking to the future and healthy growth entails being honest with yourself. If you're 45 years old and 75 pounds overweight, a goal of being a thin and vigorous 65 year old will require significant lifestyle changes...or a change in your future vision. If you feel strongly that God is nudging you to sell your possessions and live with the poor, a dream of retiring to an expensive gated community may be out of the question.

And this is exactly the point. People can certainly change and grow, but a realistic assessment of where you are and where you would like to be provides both a guide and a motivation for growth.

A friend of mine—I'll call her Anne—told me recently, "I'd give anything to look like Maria." Now Maria is one of those women who spends an inordinate amount of time and money on her grooming. Her hair is always immaculately cut, colored, and arranged. Her nail polish is never chipped. She moisturizes, exfoliates, waxes, and tones. And Maria looks great.

Anne, on the other hand, typically gives her hair and makeup a lick and a promise before running out to do what she likes to do. And that's fine. Anne is creative, industrious, and gifted, and she makes important contributions to her world. When she said she would give anything to look like Maria, I had a quick reply for her.

"No, you wouldn't."

The facts are that Anne has the same amount of time and money Maria does, but she's made other choices about how to use those resources—and she prefers the choices she's made 99.9 percent of the time.

From the time I was a young woman I've seen myself as a gray-haired teacher who derives energy and pleasure from helping younger women learn to manage their lives. For years my friends laughed at me and raised their eyebrows for even *thinking* about being old—let alone talking about it. But my vision of a lively and useful old age has shaped my decisions along the way, helped me form goals, and brought me motivation as I worked to grow into the older woman I wanted to be.

Today, by God's grace and help, I'm beginning to live out the "senior dream" I've always had for my life.

What do you use for resources on your journey? Quality teaching for growth isn't hard to find—although it may require some careful discernment. Books and magazines, courses and seminars, can supply good instruction. So can Bible study groups and mentors. If your vision of the future requires a career change or a completely new direction, you may need to go back to school.

You can find specialized help, of course…a personal trainer, a nutrition coach, or a career counselor. They can help you develop new disciplines and point you in the right direction. A sharing group may provide support, encouragement, and accountability as you seek to build new habits and break old ones. But even with such support, change basically comes down to sheer perseverance and daily reliance on God's strength.

What we most keenly need in any time of growth and stretching toward new goals is hope. If we rely on our husbands or best friends (or even our pastors or ministers) to supply that hope, we may find ourselves let down at times. But in the Lord we have a limitless supply of hope.

And what kind of hope are we talking about? Not a wispy, wimpy, wish-upon-a-star sort of fairy tale hope. Not even close! The kind of hope God offers is stronger than steel, brighter than diamonds, older than stars, deeper than the Pacific, and more sure than the morning sunrise. One New Testament writer speaks of God's kids taking refuge in Him and finding "strong encouragement to take hold of the hope set before us. This hope we have as an anchor of the soul, a hope both sure and steadfast" (Hebrews 6:18-19 NASB).

Our God is the God of hope! Hope gushes from Him like beautiful, crystal-clean water flowing from an artesian well and splashing over our lives. His desire is that you overflow with hope all the time by the power of His indwelling Holy Spirit (Romans 15:13). When you find your vision fading or evaporating before your very eyes, you need to spend some quiet, alone time with the God of hope and allow Him to refill your empty cup.

If we ask God to help us grow toward worthy goals, He will be faithful to do just that. But remember, He may also answer our prayers in ways we never, never expect. The Bible makes it clear that God's ways are not our ways, and also that God actively disciplines His daughters and sons for their own benefit. (Take some time to read Hebrews 12 on this important subject.) What this means is that growing in the Lord is partly a matter of keeping alert to what He might be doing through your circumstances.

Much as we may hate to admit it, most of us find we do our best and most productive growing in times of difficulty, loss, and conflict. We humans are a stubborn lot who often require significant discomfort and pain before getting serious about growing and changing. And our God, I've learned, can be trusted to give us what we need—even if that means kicking us out of our well-worn ruts and comfortable nests or stripping our lives of things we truly care about in order to clear the way for new growth.

If you're going through one of those times when positive change seems to elude you, when you feel restless or confused, or when you don't like where you are but don't know what to do next, I advise you to be especially watchful. Do your best to persevere in doing what you know to do. Open your heart to what God is preparing for you. As Paul wrote, "Let us not get tired of doing what is right, for after a while we will reap a harvest of blessing if we don't get discouraged and give up" (Galatians 6:9 TLB). I'm convinced that many adults are stuck because they neglect what they know about prayer and devotion and getting counsel from God's Word and His children. The quickest way for growth to wither is to get out of the habit of daily, deliberate communion with God.

I know that answers to life's dilemmas are not always clear or black and white. Believers experience times when they persist in everything they know to do and still nothing seems to happen. Sometimes that means water is flowing underground, and they are growing sturdy, long roots instead of green shoots. Patience and wisdom are called for. If you're persisting in prayer and still feel stuck, consider that God may be growing something in your life you're not aware of. You may be within inches of the greatest growth step of your life!

Youniquely Woman

The whole purpose of this book is to encourage you to become the unique, specially designed woman you are. We want you to come into your full inheritance as a loved and precious daughter of the living God. Your feelings, your thoughts, your opinions, your individual temperament, your abilities, and your as-yet-untapped potential are all gifts from God. They're important tools to help you grow and should be treated with respect and gratitude. You don't have to live by your feelings, but you need to pay attention to them and accept that they are real. And living peacefully with others doesn't mean developing a different personality or never saying what you think.

The bottom line of growth, after all, is to become the best possible version of who you are—not become someone entirely different. God would never expect a rose to grow into a beautiful gardenia. Accepting God's gift of who you are is one of the first and most important steps I know of to live life to the fullest, unique woman that you are.

From Emilie

As a young woman, wife, and mom, I didn't really know who I was. I grew up very shy with no self-worth. It was Christ and my Bob who brought me out of my shell. Learning my gifts, talents, and temperament saved me from many bad choices. As I became self-confident in Christ, I was able to trust others as well as myself.

And don't forget, my friend, in the midst of all this growing and changing be sure to extend to yourself the same grace you give to others. God does! He's always ready with a second chance, a new possibility, a surprising idea of unlooked-for opportunity.

At any season of life, He's the God who makes all things new.

Even youniquely you.

A Spirit of Loveliness

Emilie

A welcoming home is an unmistakable expression of a welcoming heart. Like a clear alpine lake reflects a perfect image of a snowcapped peak, such a home reflects the spirit and personalities of the people who create it. It's an expression of *you*. Your home should be uniquely and beautifully you...an echo of your special and personal spirit of loveliness. But if you live with other people, making your house an expression of you certainly doesn't mean you ignore your family or roommate's tastes. A welcoming home is a reflection of *everyone* who lives there, and part of its charm is the sense of diverse personalities merging to create a one-of-a-kind environment. Your music stand, your husband's Audubon prints, and your son's baseball trophy can peacefully coexist. Together they speak a welcome to anyone who visits.

Most important, however, is the welcoming attitude in your heart. This has its birth in your willingness to accept yourself as God's child and to be grateful for your place in His family—your true spiritual home. With that foundation, dear daughters, welcome becomes a way of life. You open your life to others instead of shutting them out or turning them away. You learn to see encounters with people as gifts instead of viewing them as hindrances or distractions. And you treasure your close relationships for what they are—gifts from God.

With that attitude, a smile and a hug become as vital to the spirit of welcome as a candle and a pot of stew.

Kay spoke earlier about cultivating the atmosphere of heaven within your home—a refuge from a sometimes cold and hostile outside world. I love that. The writer of Hebrews instructs: "Do not neglect to show hospitality to strangers, for by this some have entertained angels without knowing it" (Hebrews 13:2). In other words, the heavenly visitors felt right at home. They walked through the front door, sensed the atmosphere under that roof, breathed in the fragrance of love and kindness, and said, "This home reminds us of Home. It makes us think of heaven."

Of course it does! The same Jesus who makes His throne in heaven also takes up residence within the hearts of those who belong to Him and love Him. The fragrance of their lives is Christ:

From Donna

We lost our house to a flood and were displaced for a year. I longed, pined, and missed the surroundings of comfort in the early months. Slowly and steadily we returned to the activities of our former home. People came by for meals, movies, and celebrations. The spirit of loveliness comes from within.

> Thanks be to God who in Christ always leads us in triumphal procession, and through us spreads the fragrance of the knowledge of him everywhere. For we are the aroma of Christ to God among those who are being saved and among those who are perishing, to one a fragrance from death to death, to the other a fragrance from life to life (2 Corinthians 2:14-16).

Don't imagine that I'm simply playing with a nice metaphor here. The literal presence of Jesus in your home has a distinct fragrance and creates a clearly identifiable atmosphere. Just as Jesus welcomes all who come to Him for hope, for health, for grace, and for life, so your welcoming home conveys a significant blessing on those who step over your threshold.

A welcoming home is a place where you're made aware of God's blessing and through which you pass on His blessings to others. What a wonderful thought! I love what Paul wrote to the Romans. He was looking forward to an upcoming visit with the believers and said, "I know that when I come to you I will come in the fullness of the blessing of Christ" (Romans 15:29).

Paul was speaking about bringing the blessing of Christ as he entered the homes of the believers. But it can also work the other way around. When people walk through your door, when people come under your roof, you can make sure that by the time they take their leave, they've experienced "the fullness of the blessing of Christ."

As much as my husband and I love our present home, we believe it belongs to God not us. In fact, six weeks after we moved into our "Barnes beach cottage," we paid homage to that fact with a house blessing. Our church family shared dinner on the grounds, and then we stood together with our pastor for a little ceremony dedicating the property to God. Before we spent our first night in our beach house, I walked into each room and prayed a blessing upon its walls, asking that peace, joy, love, honesty, and patience would permeate the surroundings.

From Donna

Home and the loveliness of God's presence there has been the main theme of Emilie's life. She shared her wisdom with me, and now she shares it with you. My home resonates with intentional reflections of God and His presence, from the Scripture painted elegantly in the entryway to the warm use of color and light.

And God has honored our request! Our house truly has been a rich source of blessing to us and others. Since that day when we gave it back to God, we've had dinners, Bible studies, seminars, and other gatherings on the grounds.

You see, "home" is not a building. Home is not a structure of wood, brick, metal, and spackle. Home is what grows *within* the building walls and is nurtured by the hearts and souls of those who dwell together in its shelter.

Allow the joy and peace of our Lord to permeate the walls of your home and the "rooms" of your life with the true spirit of loveliness, which only Christ can give you. Open your hearts and allow your teachable spirit to develop a home and life that are filled with caring, warmth, growth…and welcome.

What other ways are there to make your home welcoming? Furnishings and décor play a big part. And this doesn't have to mean spending a lot of money. Your taste, of course, may not be anything like mine. You may prefer clean, modern lines to the chintz and china I love in our beach home. Maybe you can't live with a piano and wall-to-wall bookshelves. You may prefer chunky pottery mugs to the dainty china cups I collect and treasure.

But if you're like most women, you long for a home that is warm and welcoming, comfortable and freeing—a place where you can express the uniqueness of your God-given talents and nurture your relationships with people you love. You're hungry for a home—and a life—that reflects your personality and renews your soul. A life that glows with loveliness.

Beauty is already there, you know. I believe the spirit of loveliness resides in your heart as a woman and as a daughter of the living God. I hope the thoughts in this book, brief as they may have been, will help that loveliness shine forth wherever you live and wherever you go.

From Kay

As a young girl I would go through the house turning on lights so people would know we were home and stop to visit. In the early church believers went from house to house to share and have meals together. Why not do the same? Your house doesn't have to be perfect—the door just has to be open. People are lonely for this kind of fellowship!

"Unless the LORD Builds the House..."

Kay

Unless the LORD builds the house,
They labor in vain who build it;
Unless the LORD guards the city,
The watchman keeps awake in vain
(Psalm 127:1).

For all the collected wisdom, experience, stories, and practical ideas for living that Emilie, Donna, and I have gleaned through the years, attending our Youniquely Woman events or reading our books alone won't make a difference in your heart, your home, and your marriage. You could spend hours at your favorite bookstore scanning every book and magazine on home and marriage from every expert around the world...but in the long run, you would still come up short. I'm not being pessimistic or cynical. I'm simply telling you what God tells us in His Word: "Unless the LORD builds the house, they labor in vain who build it." Unless the living God is active in your home, in your parenting, and in your marriage, all the work and study and trying and sacrificing will get you precisely nowhere.

He is the One who invented marriage between one man and one woman for life. And this has never changed. God knows exactly how it should and must work. He is also the One who blessed the institution of marriage in His first miracle in Cana of Galilee, where He used His mighty creative power to provide for a young couple who were at the end of their resources.

As you read John 2, note that Jesus didn't step in to transform ordinary well water into fine wine until the family was against the wall and had no personal resources, nothing left to offer their guests. Moving quietly behind the scenes with no talk or fanfare, Jesus entered their life story and gave them what they could never have provided for themselves—rescuing that all-important wedding feast from humiliation and disaster.

He is still in the business of doing just that.

No matter who you are or where you are, no matter what your worries, fears, or life situation, Jesus can step into your life and turn everything around. He can use His creative power and infinite wisdom to find solutions and answers where you imagined no solutions or answers were left to be found.

From Donna

Take it from me—I tried to build a house alone. I even tried to build a house for God alone. No amount of good behavior and good habits can build a home worthy of offering to Christ. Build His way! "Let the peace of Christ rule in your heart."

In fact, unless He "builds the house," every effort you make will ultimately be in vain. But when you lay everything at His feet, seeking His help and His answers, when you humbly and diligently seek His mind and His counsel in the precepts of His timeless Word…life becomes an adventure beyond what you can imagine.

That doesn't mean everything will always come up roses, and that you won't have trouble or heartache in life. None of us gets a "pass" where human suffering and setbacks are concerned. But because our God is eternal, outside of time, He can look at our whole life story and give us the perspective and wisdom we can't come up with on our own. Emilie, Donna, and I could fill a room full of books with all He has done and undertaken in our lives and ministries.

Dear daughter, my word to you as a younique woman of God is to seek Him in His Word as never before. Learn how to observe, interpret, and apply what you read. Jack and I established Precept Ministries for precisely that reason—to help people of all ages—from children to adults—discover the truth for themselves and in doing so, find help and hope and understanding in the whole counsel of God's Word.

No matter how much you know about God's Word, if you don't apply what you've learned, Scripture will never benefit your life. To be a hearer of the Word and not a doer is to deceive yourself (James 1:22-25). This is why application of Bible truths is so vital. Observation and interpretation are the "hearing" of God's Word. With application, you'll be transformed into Christ's image. Application is the embracing of the truth, changing your mind to conform to what God says, which is absolute, unchanging truth, and then doing it. This process allows God's Spirit to work freely in your life, your marriage, your parenting, and your home.

From Donna

Kay reminds us to put first things first. And she is right. It's the Lord's faithful plan that the lives of believers be built upon His rock, not our own. The winds will not prevail against such a home...or your home.

God will build or rebuild your life as He speaks to you "line upon line, precept upon precept" from the pages of Scripture.

Friend, do you have any concept of how much God loves you? Perhaps you say, "Well, Kay, you have no idea the mistakes I've made and all my failures." It doesn't matter. I've made mistakes too. I've nearly drowned in my own failures and messes of my own making. But my heavenly Father saved me and embraced me as His very own. It doesn't matter what you've done or how far you've fallen. God's arms are open wide!

When I was a little girl I would ask my daddy, "How much do you love me?" And he would stretch out his arms as far as he could and say, "I love you *this* much." And on the cross, when they stretched the arms of our Lord Jesus wide and nailed His hands to the cross, He was saying to every one of us, "I love you *this* much" (2 Corinthians 5:21; Romans 8:31-39). Jesus says, "If you come to Me, I will make you a new woman. All the old things will pass away, and everything will become brand-new" (paraphrase of 2 Corinthians 5:17).

You truly are younique, you know. You are uniquely God's. He loves you, He died and rose again to rescue you, and He would love nothing better than to make you into a never-to-be-duplicated vessel for His glory. And how does that happen? It's a matter of faith. First, believe you are a sinner.[1] You have walked your own way, believed what you wanted to believe, and broken God's commandments. This is sin, and the payment for sin is death and separation from God for eternity.[2]

But God doesn't want you to be separated from Him; He wants you to be reconciled to Him. This is why He sent His Son into the world, born a human being but without sin, because God is His father.[3] Jesus is the Son of God.[4] He was born on earth to die for your sins. God allowed Jesus, the only human being to be born without sin, to die on a cross where He bore your sins in His body and died in your place.[5]

Jesus died.[6] He was buried.

But on the third day Jesus rose from the dead. He was resurrected because our Holy God was satisfied with His payment for your sins.[7] When you tell God you believe what He says about His Son and receive Jesus as *your* God, *your* Lord, *your* Savior, then you become a forever child of God and receive the gift of eternal life![8] Then God's Spirit comes to live in your body.[9] He's your ticket to heaven![10] Guaranteed by God. And the Spirit within also gives you the power to live a life pleasing to Him.[11]

If you want to follow God and live forever with Him, fill out this statement and talk to God. He wants to hear from you!

On this day _____ of _____, I believe![12]

And Father, this is what I want to say... (Talk to God. He's waiting to hear from you!)

Young Woman, Come Home

An Urgent Appeal

Kay

Bless you, dear daughter, for reading this book and taking these words of encouragement and counsel to heart. Emilie, Donna, and I pray our words have inspired you to glory in your uniqueness and high calling as a woman, wife, mother, and daughter of the living God.

Our book was almost finished and ready to go to press when the Lord gave me a great burden in my heart to complete this work with these last thoughts. I added this epilogue because I feel a strong sense of urgency to share with you a deeply felt appeal.

Do you remember being a teenager and heading out the door to some activity when your mother or father stopped you with one last "Be careful…" or "Be sure to…" or "Don't forget…"? Think of this last little chapter in that light. I have such a love in my heart for young women that I must give you one last bit of counsel as you close the book and head into the rest of your life.

I'm pleading with you and other young women across our nation to embrace their calling as wives and mothers. It is…

- a call to embrace the Word of God—and thus the wisdom of God—and to live according to His precepts.
- a call to embrace your husband and your children, recognizing the high calling God has placed on your life.

- a call to be used of God in these last days to turn the tide of the culture by turning the hearts of your children to the Lord.

- a call to live passionately for the one and only true God and His kingdom.

Let's take a quick step back and get some perspective on what has happened to the roles of women.

Confronting a Failed Culture

If you're feeling guilty at the thought of staying at home while your husband labors in the workplace, I have a strong word of exhortation for you: *This is misplaced guilt from the prince of this world—Satan— who desires the destruction of our lives, our marriages, and our families.* Statistics bear me out: By every measure, the American family is in deep trouble. We live in a society that is sick at heart, has lost any sense of a moral compass, and is rapidly crumbling around us.

Our country is no longer healthy or strong—physically, mentally, intellectually, morally, or emotionally. As a result we're rapidly losing our once-lofty, envied position within the family of nations. Do you realize that thousands upon thousands of children will graduate from high school this year lacking the basic skills of reading, writing, and math? Standing at the brink of adulthood, many of these young men and women are not only educationally unprepared, they are emotionally unsteady and morally weak. Why?

Because their mothers have not been home to raise them.

Because moms and dads are not parenting their children.

Many of these teens have parented themselves through life, with little guidance, discipline, or encouragement at home. How will these young men and women know what to do when it's their turn to be parents?

Please permit me, an older woman, to take you back in history for a moment. In the middle years of the last century, even as the external threat of communism confronted free nations all over the world, many predicted that America's greatest danger would come from within.

Because of moral decay and the collapse of the family, America would simply implode, much as the Roman Empire did 2,000 years ago.

How can we prevent this from happening? How can our great democracy—founded as it was on biblical principles—recover? Here's where you come in, precious daughter.

Our country—our beloved America—is only as strong as her families. If our families continue to fail, no political manipulations, no military service, no weapons—nuclear or otherwise—can save us. But as a woman, wife, and mother—you are the God-ordained glue of the family. You can make an impact.

Three Destructive Lies

I personally believe we're headed where we are as a people because we've largely bought into three lies that have deeply wounded our nation and culture. And each of these lies can be tied to a specific person. Maybe you've heard of them and maybe you haven't. I bring them up to help you understand how we arrived at where we currently stand.

Julius Wellhausen: "The Bible Is Irrelevant"

The first lie blew in like a toxic cloud on a wind out of Germany in the 1870s. It was a direct attack on what was being taught in our nation's universities and seminaries. Do you see Satan's strategy here? He attacked the church of Jesus Christ by invading the very seminaries where young men were being trained to pastor and shepherd the flock of God.

This movement began as most do, with one man's outrageous notions that began to shape the opinions of others. In this case the man was Julius Wellhausen, a German rationalist, intellectual, Old Testament scholar, and theologian, who came to the conclusion that human reasoning was totally trustworthy—and the Bible wasn't!

Until the time of Wellhausen and the German rationalists, people believed without question that the Bible could be trusted—that it was the Word of God. Wellhausen insisted otherwise. In his estimation the Bible was simply a collection of human documents compiled by men, while the events of the Old Testament were nothing more than a product of evolutionary thinking. Wellhausen called for a "new understanding" of the nature of truth and revelation in the pages of the Bible.

The result? The truth of the Bible was first doubted and then denied outright. And a cold, godless rationalism slipped in like a shadow to take its place.

Here's the problem. When you throw out the revelation of God, when you make the revealed truth of Scripture into a book of myths and fairy tales, you no longer have a plumb line of truth. You're left without standards, without directions, without ethics, and without road signs on the path of life.

For the first time in history people doubted the inerrancy of God's Word. Those who bought into this lie lost their moral compass. *And that is exactly where we are today in our public schools and secular universities.* This is why you as a parent need to bring up your children on the Word of God—and why you must teach your sons and daughters how to discover truth for themselves.[1] At a very early age we put a spoon in the hand of a toddler, teaching him how to feed himself. We must do the same with the Word of God, teaching young hearts and minds how to draw life-giving and life-shaping truths from its pages.

How can we say we "don't have time" to study the Bible or teach it to our children? God's Word contains the very essence of life by which we measure all of life! Without a strong knowledge of and faith in the great truths and precepts of Scripture, we're lost in a dangerous wilderness with no compass. God's Word is the map of truth by which we navigate all we believe and do.

Yes, many of us could provide materially for our children's every need, pay their way through college, and even shower them with love and affection...but if we neglect to teach them God's Word and God's ways, we fail in the most important parenting task of all.

Alfred Kinsey: "Sexual Morality Is Unnecessary"

Some say our culture has become completely immoral. But I say we are no longer moral and no longer immoral. We've become *amoral.* There are no rights and no wrongs. What is truth for me (we're told) may not be truth for you. So everyone does what is right in his or her own eyes.

In the fifth century Augustine wrote that Christians opposed the unrestrained sexual lifestyle of the Romans and were despised for it.[2] Tertullian said Romans so despised believers that they hated the very name "Christian."[3]

Christianity prompted the Western world to outlaw adultery, pedophilia, homosexuality, and bestiality. Not so very long ago there were laws across the United States that forbade these activities and more. Some of these laws still remain as statutes in local governments, but they're no longer enforced. In fact, they're usually ridiculed.

In 1948 the infamous Kinsey Report, with its pseudoscientific findings on the sexuality of men and women, resulted in the repealing of laws against numerous sexual misbehaviors laid out in the Bible. Kinsey, the father of the sexual revolution, despised the Word of God, declaring deviant sexual behavior normal. To this day Kinsey is still cited in "case law"—replacing the truth of the Scriptures.

So where was the church as Wellhausen invaded our education system and Kinsey trashed our nation's sexual morals? Did we roll up our sleeves and say this is not going to be? Some believers did. Many did not. More and more churches were swept along in the popular current that made science king and believed all of mankind's problems, hurts, and perplexities could be resolved by psychology and the teachings of Sigmund Freud. But psychology was a poor substitute for *Jehovah Rapha,* the God who heals.

Tired of the reproach and suffering that comes with identification with Christ, liberal churches, thinking themselves "freed" from the absolutes of Scripture and directed by their feelings, boarded a cruise ship and took a vacation with the world. Members slept in the world's bed, committing acts of immorality.

A great many in "the church" universal (note I said "universal"— there is a faithful remnant, and I am not referring to them) became like the church of Laodicea in the book of Revelation (3:14-20). Their deeds were neither cold nor hot, but lukewarm. It made God want to vomit. It still does.

Betty Friedan: "Home and Family Can Take Second Place"

In 1963, on her forty-second birthday, Betty Friedan published *The Feminine Mystique.* Although she never used the word *feminism* in her book, her writings ignited the feminist movement and birthed NOW, the National Organization of Women. Friedan spoke about "the problem that has no name," which she identified as the yearning of women to be something more than moms and homemakers. Of the American woman at mid-century she wrote, "As she made the beds, shopped for groceries, matched slipcover material, ate peanut butter sandwiches with her children, chauffeured Cub Scouts and Brownies, lay beside her husband at night, she was afraid to ask even of herself the silent question: 'Is this all?' "[4]

"Is *this* all?" How similar in implication to the words of the serpent when he implied there was more to be had if Eve would but eat what God had forbidden!

As a result of 50-plus years of feminist influence and thinking, for the first time in the history of the United States the majority of adult women participate in the labor market. Men are no longer the sole providers for their families. But is this what's best for the children, the families, our nation? You only have to look at the status of our society, read the statistics compiled by George Barna and others, and you have the answer. We are destroying ourselves from within.

You and I must rise to the call back to biblical truth and urge others to join us before our once-great nation falls from the inside out. There is much we can do as women if we make the Bible our primary textbook for life and trust God to support our obedience to His call. If we fulfill our God-ordained calling and purpose and make our husbands and children our priorities, the Lord will bless our families and our country.

Longing for a Soft Touch

A number of years ago a college student showed me an article in his psychology textbook.[5] I was captivated by what I read and torn by a picture of a little baby monkey curled up in fear. This was a monkey "raised" by two surrogate mothers. One was an artificial mother made of wire cylinders, a wooden head, and an attached bottle that substituted for a breast. It was just a framework with no padding, no softness. The other surrogate mother had no bottle attached, but was wrapped with soft terry cloth.

When the little monkey felt frightened or threatened, guess which mother he wanted to cling to? The one with the soft cozy cloth! When he was hungry, he simply leaned over to the wire mother to get his milk—still clinging to the soft mamma. The author of this textbook explained, "In human infants, too, attachment usually grows from body contact with parents who are soft and warm and who rock, feed, and pat. No social behavior is more striking than this intense infant love, called *attachment,* a powerful survival impulse that keeps infants close to their caregivers."

What difference does a nurturing parent make? I have in my files a pamphlet that is a collection of excerpts from papers by Armand M. Nicholi, Jr. of Harvard Medical School. Let me bullet some of his statements:

- A vast body of research during more than four decades led the World Health Organization to make this statement: "What is believed to be essential for mental health is that the infant and young child should experience a warm, intimate, and continuous relationship with his mother."

- No human interaction has greater impact on our lives than our family experience.

- The breakdown of the family contributes significantly to the major problems confronting our society today. Research data make unmistakably clear a strong relationship between broken families and the drug epidemic, the increase in out-of-wedlock pregnancies, the rise in violent crime, and the unprecedented epidemic of suicide among children and adolescents.

- Can one make any general statement concerning the relationship between presence or absence of parents and the emotional health of their children? If any one factor influences the character development and emotional stability of an individual, it is the quality of the relations he experiences as a child with his parents.

- We use the cliché "it's the quality and not the quantity of time that counts." But time and emotional accessibility are like the oxygen we breathe. Although the quality of the oxygen is important, the quantity determines whether we live or die. *A parent's inaccessibility physically, emotionally or both, can exert a profound influence on a child's emotional health.*[6]

Please hear me on this, precious one: There is *no* substitute for mother at home, and mom and dad under the same roof with their children. If I'd known these truths I would never have listened to the two seminary trained and ordained "counselors" who advised me to leave my first husband. How I wish they would have introduced me to the Son of God and the Word of God! (This is why it's such a privilege to share my insights with you!)

Neither our temporal, immediate happiness nor the fulfillment of our self-centered desires is worth the long-term consequences of ignoring God's precepts for life. As you've seen, God ordained the family, which begins with a husband and wife and then, as God wills, children. His pattern, as we've discovered, is for the mother to be the keeper of the home, the father to be the breadwinner, and both to be involved in the parenting of the children.

Please take a careful look at this passage and underline every instance of the word *when*.

> These words, which I am commanding you today, shall be on your heart. You shall teach them diligently to your sons and shall talk of them when you sit in your house and when you walk by the way and when you lie down and when you rise up (Deuteronomy 6:6-7).

This passage is directed to the father—the parent primarily responsible for the spiritual nurturing of the children (a truth affirmed in Ephesians 6). Look at the *whens* you underlined. Does that sound like an absentee father? No! It's a father who is present and active!

Dr. Armand Nicholi Jr. says, "A child experiences an absent or an emotionally inaccessible parent as rejection, and rejection inevitably breeds resentment and hostility. Depending on the age of the child, particular emotional makeup of the child, and the sex of the parent who is missing or inaccessible, the child, when he becomes an adult, may experience various kinds of crippling emotional conflict."[7]

A loving, stable home—rich or poor—where both parents are actively involved in the lives of their children day in and day out is the best environment for nurturing emotionally healthy and socially stable individuals. This is extremely hard to accomplish if both parents are working. When mothers work outside the home it puts added stress on family life. We can't "do it all," and we shouldn't try. When we attempt to, tension enters the home at levels beyond what God intended.

When mother works outside the home, the lives of the children become far more structured, leaving little time for leisure and creativity. Children have to get up earlier because mom and dad have to be out of the house to get to work on time. And because mom is not at home, provision has to be made for the care of the children after school or during work hours for toddlers. No more coming home to mom and the smell of baked cookies. To someone to talk to, to help with homework, to welcome with open arms and listening ears.

When mothers went to work outside the home, family life was greatly changed. One senior research scientist wrote, "There is a time crunch in families...Kids are leading much more hectic lives, their time carefully parceled out among school, after-school care, soccer, ballet, karate, piano, horseback riding, and 'play dates' with less time not only for pure play but also for family meals and even simple conversation within families."[8]

When families don't sit around the table for meals together, "family communication and family closeness seems to be getting downplayed and the role of activity participation has gotten ampli-fied."⁹ The article I'm citing suggests we're trying to give our children everything…everything but ourselves and our time.

From Emilie

We've shared so much wisdom with you eager women. We're calling you to come home, raise your children, and be the Proverbs 31 woman who watches carefully all that goes on throughout her household. You've learned how to love and follow God, establish a welcoming home, set a table, create family memories, and honor and respect your husband. I pray you'll continue to seek God, to grow, to love your husband and family, and to reach out to others. May God bless you!

You, dear reader, are the glue of the family—the substance that holds the lives of your children together. You have a God-ordained career laid out for you by your Creator. Strive to get your AUG degree: "Approved unto God." Live life God's way, and you will have no regrets.

Please look beyond today to tomorrow. Develop a long-range vision and let long-term goals discipline your desire for immediate fulfillment. Remember, children grow up fast, and there will be time for other things in later years. Invest in your sons and daughters while they're under your roof and direct guidance. Shape these young lives for their best and God's glory. Don't subcontract that infinitely precious task to others. Then, no matter what course your children may take in future years, you'll have a good conscience because you followed the priorities of God's Word.

Benjamin Rush, a signer of the Declaration of Independence and an educator, said, "Mothers and schools plant the seeds of nearly all the good and evil which exists in the world today." Open your arms, Mother, and embrace your calling. Each child has been given to you by Almighty God, and in all of eternity, you will never have another opportunity like this!

Notes

Chapter 1—Living Intentionally

1. Quote by Amelia Hudson Boomhall, source unknown, written as explanatory text in a museum.

Chapter 2—A Vision for Home

1. I (Kay) highly recommend Devi Titus and Marilyn Weiher's book *The Home Experence: Making Your Home a Sactuary and a Haven of Peace* (Ohio: Living Smart Resources, 2007), www.livingsmartresources.com.

Chapter 3—Modeling a Balanced Life

1. Dan Sullivan, *The 21-Day Time Breakthrough*.
2. Daniel Goleman, *Social Intelligence*.
3. 1 Corinthians 13:7-8; 14:1.

Chapter 4—Building a Marriage Without Regrets

1. Dr. J.H. Hertz, CH, ed., *The Pentateuch and Haftorahsi* (London: Soncino Press, 5755/1994), p. 9.
2. www.thatwasfunny.com.
3. Shaunti Feldhahn, "How to Know What You Don't Know About Sex," *Mtl* magazine, March–April 2006, p. 65.
4. Dr. Mark Goulston, quoted in *Reader's Digest,* Oct. 2005, p. 105.
5. Ibid.
6. Kay Arthur, *The Truth About Sex* (Colorado Springs: Waterbrook Press, 2002, 2005).

Chapter 5—Parenting with Purpose

1. Dr. Gleason Archer, *Encyclopedia of Bible Difficulties* (Grand Rapids: Zondervan Publishing House, 1982), p. 252.
2. Timothy R. Jennings, M.D., *Could It Be This Simple? A Biblical Model for Healing the Mind* (Hagerstown, MD: Autumn House Publishing, 2007), p. 34.
3. Lawrence Epstein, "The Magic Power of Sleep," *Reader's Digest,* Oct. 2007, p. 112.
4. Proverbs 12:25; 15:13 niv; 15:30 niv; 17:22.

Chapter 6—Nurturing Your Spiritual Life

1. For a more complete discussion of prayer, read chapter 13, "Making Time for Prayer," in Donna Otto, *Secrets to Getting More Done in Less Time* (Eugene, OR: Harvest House Publishers, 1995).

Chapter 8—Continuing the Adventure

1. Romans 3:10-18,23.

2. Romans 6:23.

3. Matthew 1:18-23.

4. John 20:30-31.

5. 1 John 4:9-10; Romans 5:6-8, 10-11; 2 Corinthians 5:21.

6. 1 Peter 1:18-19.

7. Romans 4:25; 1 Corinthians 15:3-8.

8. John 1:12; 3:16-18,36.

9. Ephesians 1:13-14; 1 Corinthians 6:19-20; 2 Corinthians 5:17; Romans 8:16-17; 1 John 5:11-13.

10. Romans 8:23.

11. Galatians 5:16-25.

12. 1 Thessalonians 2:13. We're so excited for you! Love Emilie, Donna, and Kay.

An Urgent Appeal

1. For solid advice and encouragement, read Donna Otto, *Loving Life as an At-Home Mom.* For your kids, check out the Discover 4 Yourself Inductive Bible Studies for children written by Kay Arthur and Janna Arndt and offered through Precept Ministries, precept.org, 800-763-8280, and in Christian bookstores. The studies are excellent and full of puzzles, activities, and biblical truth.

2. Alvin J. Schmidt, *Under the Influence: How Christianity Transformed Civilization* (Grand Rapids, MI: Zondervan Publishing House, 2001), p. 94, citing Augustine, *City of God.*

3. Tertullian, *Apology 3,* in ibid.

4. Harold Evans, *The American Century* (New York: Alfred A Knopf, 2000), pp. 596-97.

5. David G. Myers, *Exploring Psychology,* 2nd ed. (New York: Worth Publishers, 1993), pp. 71-77.

6. Armand M. Nicholi, Jr., MD, "What Do We Know About Successful Families?" Harvard Medical School, Massachusetts General Hospital, pamphlet of excerpts from papers delivered during the past few years, n.d.

7. Ibid.

8. Sandra Hofferth, a senior research scientist at the University of Michigan's Institute for Social Research and coauthor with Jack Sandberg, of "Changes in American Children's Time, 1981–1997," *American Demographics,* May 1999, pp. 56-60.

9. Ibid., p. 60.

Graduates of the First Youniquely Woman Conference.

Harvest House Books by Kay Arthur

Discover the Bible for Yourself
God, Are You There?
God, Help Me Experience More of You
God, How Can I Live?
How to Study Your Bible
Israel, My Beloved
Lord, Teach Me to Pray in 28 Days
Lord, Teach Me to Study the Bible in 28 Days
A Marriage Without Regrets
A Marriage Without Regrets Study Guide
Speak to My Heart, God
With an Everlasting Love
Youniquely Woman

Bibles

The New Inductive Study Bible (NASB)

Discover 4 Yourself® Inductive Bible Studies for Kids

God, What's Your Name?
How to Study Your Bible for Kids
Lord, Teach Me to Pray for Kids
God's Amazing Creation (Genesis 1–2)
Digging Up the Past (Genesis 3–11)
Abraham—God's Brave Explorer (Genesis 11–25)
Extreme Adventures with God (Isaac, Esau, and Jacob)
Joseph—God's Superhero (Genesis 37–50)
You're a Brave Man, Daniel (Daniel 1–6)
Fast-Forward to the Future (Daniel 2,7–12)
Wrong Way, Jonah! (Jonah)
Jesus in the Spotlight (John 1–11)
Jesus—Awesome Power, Awesome Love (John 11–16)
Jesus—To Eternity and Beyond! (John 17–21)
Boy, Have I Got Problems! (James)
Bible Prophecy for Kids (Revelation 1–7)
A Sneak Peek into the Future (Revelation 8–22)

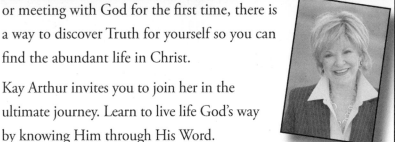

Women find value in marriage, motherhood and creating a home at Homemakers By Choice.

Listen to Donna Otto's daily podcast!

Homemakers By Choice

Homemakers By Choice is a non-profit, faith-based organization designed to support and encourage stay-at-home moms.

To learn more, please visit us on our website:

www.homemakersbychoice.org

888-882-7252

Donna Otto
Homemakers By Choice
11453 N. 53rd Place
Scottsdale, AZ 85254
480-991-7464

Home
Makers
BY CHOICE

Harvest House Books by Donna Otto

Finding a Mentor, Being a Mentor

Finding Your Purpose as a Mom

Loving Life as an At-Home Mom

Secrets of Getting More Done in Less Time

Harvest House Books by Emilie Barnes

15-Minute Devotions for Couples

The 15-Minute Organizer

15 Minutes Alone with God

15 Minutes of Peace with God

15 Minutes with God for Grandma

500 Time-Saving Hints for Women

Be My Refuge, Lord

Emilie's Creative Home Organizer

Heal My Heart, Lord

If Teacups Could Talk

I Need Your Strength, Lord

A Little Book of Manners

A Little Book of Manners for Boys

A Little Hero in the Making

A Little Princess in the Making

Meet Me Where I Am, Lord

Minute Meditations for Couples

More Faith in My Day

The Quick-Fix Home Organizer

Quiet Moments for a Busy Mom's Soul

A Quiet Refuge

Safe in the Father's Hands

Simple Secrets to a Beautiful Home

A Tea to Comfort Your Soul

To contact Emilie or for information about
More Hours in My Day time-management
and organizational seminars, go to:

www.EmilieBarnes.com

or contact

More Hours in My Day
2150 Whitestone Dr.
Riverside, CA 92506

(951) 682-4714